ABOUT DESIGN

Ken Baynes

Design Council Publications

About Design
First edition published 1976
Design Council Publications
28 Haymarket London SW1Y 4SU

Designed by Gill Streater
Printed and bound by
Hazell Watson & Viney Ltd
Aylesbury Bucks
Distributed by
Heinemann Educational Books Ltd
48 Charles Street London W1X 8AH

ISBN 0 435 58064 7 (paperback)
     0 435 58063 9 (hardback)
© Ken Baynes 1976

Endpapers
Drawings by fifth year pupils at Pimlico School, produced as part of the Front Door project organised in the school by Eileen Adams.
(Inner London Education Authority)

Contents

For KATE, POLLY and TOM
who have made me think hard about
what it means for people to have to
live and grow up in the kind of
man-made world that exists today

Preface

by **Lord Esher** CBE DLitt PPRIBA

Rector and Vice-Provost
Royal College of Art

I have sometimes wondered why it is that the literature of architecture is so rich, while the literature of design, which embraces architecture, is so poor. Historically of course architecture (which included its setting, the garden and the park) was on its own – an art, the art of building for show. Like literature itself, it was strictly for the tiny educated elite. Everything else made by human hands, from buildings to jewellery, was craft, handed down orally, needing no literature. So it's only since the Victorians suddenly realised the crafts were collapsing that design has had a literature at all.

But there's another reason, I think, for its inadequacy: the subject is fuzzy at the edges. Once you broaden the definition of design – and you have no alternative – to mean, let's say, 'the conscious pre-determination of the human environment', you are into planning, into economics, into politics. No wonder there's puzzlement in educational circles. No wonder Ken Baynes has written this book.

For the subject is there, and it is not going to go away. Everybody can now see that the three Rs are not enough, that the more literate and numerate we get, the worse we seem to be at the ordinary good housekeeping without which we are going to destroy our habitat, that it's urgent to give educational space to this most ancient and benign of human activities – the urge to make things, to make a home, to think ahead. It's this ability to put things together, to deal in relationships, which distinguishes the designer from the scientist and the technologist, who only have to imagine, to test and to communicate.

Because of its concern with relationships, and because of its experimental character, design in general education has the unique quality of being a joint enterprise in which teachers and pupils learn together and have the fun of using their critical faculties together. There are no right answers, only right questions, and in the end good thinking.

For the purpose of course is not to educate young designers, but to educate a society and finally a world that can design itself, and so perhaps save itself. As a fellow worker in his field, and writing from a college which has a national and indeed international role in it, I am delighted that Ken Baynes has given us in this book the fruits of his special and perhaps unique experience.

Introduction

During 1974 and 1975 I was working as a research fellow at the Royal College of Art. A small team of us were engaged in a study of 'Design in General Education'. The research was sponsored by the Department of Education and Science and it took me to teachers' meetings in many parts of England and Wales. Two things struck me at once. The first was that a very large number of teachers from a variety of subject backgrounds were engaged in teaching children about design. The second was that these same teachers had only a small experience of design on which to base their approach. Confusion was rife. The inevitable prelude to any discussion was 'what do we mean by design?' and it was evident that this question reflected a deep-seated anxiety. The questioner longed for a short and clear answer, but inevitably – because the question is a subtle one – no such answer proved to be possible. The present book is an attempt to suggest ways of finding an answer that teachers will find relevant to their particular situation.

An answer? Certainly not an answer in the sense of a two-sentence definition of 'design'. I do not believe that a definition of this kind is likely to prove of lasting value, however attractive it might appear in the short run. Rather, the intention is to provide signposts pointing to a number of routes along which

teachers are likely to find it worth while to travel. The assumption is that in taking a variety of routes the beginnings of an answer will appear.

A teacher needs to be reasonably fluent in a subject if he or she is to use it as an effective medium for education. This implies confidence and familiarity built up over a period of time, and this in turn implies the willingness to make a definite effort to study and to experiment with new or unfamiliar teaching methods. I have assumed such a willingness on the part of the reader. It should be possible to use the book as a starting point for further reading and for work in the classroom. In the course of, say, three years, a substantial body of experience could be created in this way by a group or an individual.

The answer with which the book deals therefore consists not of closed definitions but of discussions of an assorted bundle of concepts, procedures and queries that seem to be of significance in any attempt to understand the present nature of design – particularly when it is seen from the viewpoint of the school and the community.

To an extent the selection of topics for detailed treatment is personal. This is because I have deliberately emphasised those things that have concerned me and with which I have been directly involved. There is, as a result, an unusual emphasis on the cultural significance of design activity, on design for health care, and on that thing which is sometimes called 'public participation' but which I prefer to call democracy.

Because of an interest in history, I tend to emphasise the historical context of design. I believe that this is one of the best ways to make a coherent picture out of what might otherwise appear to be a hopeless jumble of disconnected developments. But it is important to remember that the particular selection of topics is of less significance than the various procedures that are suggested for handling them. It is the concepts and procedures that are intended to be the useful signposts. They should be capable of being applied across a very wide range of school situations.

There is a final point to make about the book. It is not, in any sense, a manual on design education. It is not even an introduction to the topic of design in general education. Books on these themes exist and our own study at the Royal College of Art attempted to make a contribution to both of them. Here the intention is different. The aim is to provide a useful book for those whose main interest in design is that it can be used as a valuable medium for general education. The subject is design. The audience is the teacher. I hope that this book may help to make clear what it is that design has to offer in the classroom.

Ken Baynes
Whiteshill
September 1975

Chapter 1

Developments in design education

It would be easy to assume that the study of 'design' is a very new import into the school curriculum. At the time of writing (1975), the term 'design education' in connexion with secondary schools does not appear to be more than ten years old, and it is only during the last five or six years that 'design departments' or 'faculties' have come into existence. Even now there are relatively few courses devoted to training teachers specifically in 'design'. It is a subject area somewhat lacking in nationally available examinations and there is still no coherent pattern of studies linking design in general education with the requirements of the related professions of engineering, architecture and industrial design. Even less is there a clear picture of the value that design studies might have in the education of non-specialists. All this work is still to be completed. Surely this indicates that the theme is a novel one? In one sense it does, but at another more fundamental level, it does not.

It can be convincingly argued that 'design education' is simply the most recent form of one of the oldest concerns of education. It is a particular response to the conditions in which we now live, but this does not mean that education in the past ignored design. Education has always concerned itself with material culture as well as with literary and scientific culture. If specific labels are ignored, it is easy to see that what is today known as design education can trace its ancestry back to mankind's very first attempts to create shelter, tools, images and utensils. Looked at in this perspective, formal design education is as old as the earliest efforts made by artists and craftsmen to explain to those not enrolled in the 'mystery' what it was that they were trying to do.

Plato included something akin to design education in his *Republic*. He saw it in a very modern light, regarding it as an aspect of study that would mould the character and help the individual to healthy development. Here is part of the relevant dialogue:

'Good literature, therefore, and good music and beauty of form generally all depend on goodness of character; I don't mean that lack of awareness of the world which we politely call "goodness", but a character of real judgement and principle.'

'I quite agree.'

'And are not these things which our young men must try to acquire, if they are to perform their function in life properly?'

'They must.'

'And they are to be seen in painting and similar arts, in weaving and embroidery, in architecture and furniture, and in living things, animals and plants. For in all of these we find beauty and ugliness. And ugliness of form and disharmony are akin to bad art and bad character, and their opposites are akin to and represent good character and discipline.'*

* The 'Republic' (Penguin Classics), Plato, translated by H D P Lee, Penguin Books, 1955.

STROUD AND WHITESHILL

Shelter

Tom's map of Whiteshill (now the author's home village) in Gloucestershire. It shows how the village relates to Stroud, the railway station, the fish and chip shop and other important local landmarks. The map was started at the point marked

The illustrations to the first chapter are all by the author's son, Tom. They were done when he was aged six. The point of them is to demonstrate some of the basic content of design and design education: to show how fundamental is a concern with shelter, tools, images and utensils.

HOME and was then drawn out by following the experience of travelling along each road. The 'scale' is the scale of Tom's daily life in the setting of houses, fields and shops; the world that man has created by his design activity.

The sections on education in the *Republic* dealt with the proper training of an elite – a ruling oligarchy of wise men, the existence of which Plato believed to be essential if anarchy was to be avoided. This is a significant point of emphasis because, in the majority of past societies, it was only the aristocracy who could afford an education that attempted to enlarge taste and discrimination by didactic means. However, we should not imagine that this meant that the unlettered were therefore lacking in taste and discrimination. The evidence points rather the other way, and the reasons for this are important for our own teaching. Formal design education, in the sense of an explanation in words, was always the least important part of the story. Words were the least used of all the tools for communication that were available. The transmission of knowledge about material culture never depended primarily on speech or writing. Material culture was not something that affected men only when they consciously thought or spoke about it; rather it provided an all-embracing ambience in which they lived. In a strictly literal sense, it provided a structure for existence. Men and women grew up in it, played in it, worked in it. Before the Industrial Revolution, the main medium for general education in design was, quite simply, the formative experience gained from using the buildings and products made by the craftsmen of the period. It was direct knowledge transmitted by touch and sight and, in a relatively static world, it was entirely adequate for its purpose.

In many senses the knowledge of techniques and materials gained in this way was on a firmer footing than anything that could ever be obtained from books. Certainly the appreciation that people then had of making and building appears to have been deeper and more instinctive than our own. The evidence for this is everywhere to be seen in the buildings and products that remain from the times when the majority of men were illiterate and did not go to school to receive their knowledge and experience. What they made frequently displays an aesthetic competence and understanding of materials that are in advance of anything that our own more sophisticated abilities have made possible.

Recognising this fact leaves contemporary educators with a problem because, clearly, it will not do to romanticise the past. We need to be highly discriminating in our efforts to disentangle the various strands that allowed much vernacular building to be so good. To look back on peasant communities, for example, as if people lived then in some kind of perpetual summer holiday world of cottages, peace and simplicity is seriously to distort the desperation and narrow horizons of such an existence. In his book on the middle ages in Europe* Morris Bishop draws a picture which seems nearer to the truth:

Thus the medieval peasant lived, familiar with the earth, responsive to its rhythms. Alvarus Pelagius said, 'even as they plough and dig the earth all day long, so they become altogether earthy; they lick the

* *'The Penguin Book of the Middle Ages', Morris Bishop, Penguin Books, 1971.*

earth, eat the earth, they speak of the earth; in the earth they have reposed all their hopes, nor do they care a jot for the heavenly substance that shall remain'. The peasant aged rapidly and died young. His skin was hard and leathery, having been dried by exposure to all weathers and cured like a ham in the smoke of his home.

It was on the shoulders of these people, or people very much like them, that the development of vernacular buildings and utensils all over the world first depended. It was on their toil that cathedrals and temples were raised and palaces were built. They were people who knew little more of the world than what they needed to know in order to survive. When we recognise the splendid quality of much that was made in and around these circumstances, it is easy to fall into the trap of confusing poverty and subsistence with a special kind of innocent wisdom. That this is not the significant connexion is shown by the persistence of the same qualities into periods and places of relatively widespread wealth and prosperity – Gloucestershire, for example, when the wool trade was at its height. No, the kernel of what was effective in the direct 'design education' of the ages before the Industrial Revolution and the spread of formal schooling was not the existence of poverty but the simple fact of directness: real contact between hand and eye and the products of a stable tradition of building and making.

Here we are faced, for the first time, with what will be a recurrent theme in this book. Time and again, we shall look at the Industrial Revolution to find in it a watershed marking off the predominantly rural past from the predominantly urban present. In the

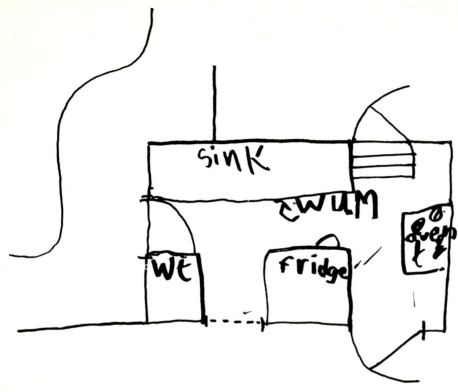

Shelter
Tom's plan for rebuilding the author's kitchen.

case of design education the contrast is particularly dramatic. Not only has education in design become – like most other education – partly a matter of formal schooling, but the stable traditions on which a sense of materials and craftsmanship previously depended have been swept away by industrialisation. Because of its essentially non-literary, non-verbal character, craftsmanship and the moral and ethical values it represents have only been fitted uncomfortably into the kind of schools that have developed since the nineteenth century.

This situation is somewhat ironic. Throughout the nineteenth century philosophers and critics worried over the standards of industrially produced goods and the newly built urban environment. From one standpoint or another, they attacked what was being made and looked to education as a means of improvement. Government itself intervened in professional design education and created the art and design schools forty years before

the passing of the 1870 Education Act. But by the time craft and design education came to be widely practised in schools it was already strictly compartmentalised, stratified, rigid and removed from contact with any vivid, living tradition. It had become boring, unrealistic and unconnected with joy.

Between the two World Wars there was in this area, as elsewhere, a great movement towards freedom and creativity. The revolution in art education is well known: it laid the foundation for the vivid painting and sculpture now found in primary and secondary schools. There was also a less well known, but equally significant, change of emphasis in craft education, or 'manual training' as it was then called. When I was preparing this book, I wrote to a number of people who had played a significant role in the growth of design education to ask them to give me an assessment of the most important factors in its development. I asked them, particularly, to do this from a personal point of view: I wanted to know what had affected them. Don Porter, who at the end of his career was Chief Inspector for Handicraft, recalled strongly contrasting school experiences when he was a pupil, student and teacher in the 1920s. Here is what he wrote:

Pre Hadow (before 1926)
I began workshop and science classes as a pupil in a selective Central school, but as our practical rooms were not ready, we started these subjects in the Technical Institute. Boys went there one day a week for a morning in the workshop and an afternoon in the laboratory. The woodwork course followed the old Manual Training scheme as interpreted

by the senior teacher of the Institute, who also doubled as organiser for craft centres in the district. The course we followed was formal in the extreme: everybody made the same things at the same time until some fell so far behind that they had to be treated separately. It really was training; we did planing by numbers and learned the parts of tools by rote, just as our teachers had learned the parts of the rifle and the machine gun not so long before. We worked our way through marble boards, key racks, pot stands and so on, up to simple frame jobs – like the firescreen – and some not so simple – like the Oxford frame. I still have some of these 'models' as we always called them. Technically the teaching was effective and those with reasonable manual skill and tidiness covered a lot of ground in a couple of years. We also had theory lessons about tools and timbers, and drawing lessons which consisted of copying teacher's drawings line by line from the blackboard. If the word design was mentioned at all it was always in relation to shape and ornament; we 'designed' the back of some object, the curved top of the firescreen or its feet. Another weakness was that craft was taught in isolation from other subjects, even from science which was taught just across the corridor.

Post Hadow (after 1926)
After just over two years at the Institute our own practical block was completed and although the workshop was very small and cramped, the effect was dramatic. In part this was because we were in our own premises, but the teacher was now free to develop his own ideas. Nobody talked of integration, or even of correlation, which was then the 'with it' term, but we linked up with science, art and mathematics and to a lesser extent with geography, history and domestic science. This was feasible because less time was spent on basic instruction, which was still taken seriously, leaving more time for group and individual work. Boys who

wished could learn some metalwork also, but not under very good conditions; metal was useful when it came to making apparatus for subjects such as science or geography.

From the design point of view we were moving in the right direction and I remember sketches passing to and from the workshop for discussion. The science master was always devising new things for the school; he made radio sets and a plywood loudspeaker so that we could listen to the very first radio broadcasts to schools. But when we made things for the laboratory, the craft teacher wanted them made to a fairly high standard and he was not pleased when he saw them drilled with fresh holes and modified out of recognition. We also worked closely with the art teacher, for example in carving wood blocks for fabric printing, but some of the shapes we attempted were too difficult in the materials we used. Thus many of the difficulties we have since experienced with integration were already there, especially the concern over 'craftsmanship'. For example, when we worked in the laboratory to 'make a telescope', was it to be a quick job made with cardboard tubes and sealing wax, or a gleaming brass instrument that would take far longer to make?

During this period great progress was made in schools that were reorganised and it came as something of a shock to find so many all-age schools continuing even into the early sixties. In retrospect however one can see the impact of a concerted drive by inspectors, lecturers and advisers and especially of the Board of Education's 'Circus', as the short local courses were known. The first specialist HMIs for Handicraft were appointed in the 1920s, but many general inspectors also saw the crafts as a keystone in the curriculum of the new senior schools. The emphasis on the basic scheme was still there but it was to be shorter and more concerned with construction; hence small furniture making became the order of the

day, much of it made to standard designs, but allowing for individual variants. Some very useful books appeared about furniture making, tools and apparatus for various purposes. Another influence was the appointment of consultant designers at Shoreditch and Loughborough, resulting from a Board of Trade inquiry into standards of design. A recommendation by this committee made it possible for practising designers like John Farleigh, Peter Waals and later Edward Barnsley to influence the training of teachers. In the schools the word design began to be used more meaningfully and people lectured and wrote books about it. The project method of teaching also made good progress in some areas, leading to a more profitable type of apparatus making, some of it with an approach that anticipated Project Technology in our own time.

It must be remembered that good materials were easy to get and not too expensive in pre-war days. Things could be made cheaply in the schools that were welcome in the homes. Good quality deal was available for garden and kitchen equipment, but mahogany, black walnut, Japanese oak and American whitewood could all be obtained in clean, seasoned boards. This factor undoubtedly influenced the development of the crafts in schools and accounted for the predominance of furniture making.

It is easy to recognise in this description the origins of many later approaches to design education. Clearly the old manual training was unsatisfactory, both in relation to the developing body of liberal educational theory and to the realities of an industrial world undergoing rapid economic and social change. The pressure was already on the teacher to respond. The sequence of change and development in which we are still working was beginning in the 1920s and 1930s but it was dramatically accelerated by the experience of the Second World War. The new sense of classlessness and unity of national purpose that this produced led to a series of social reforms as great as any that have ever been attempted in Britain. For education, the climactic moment was the passing into law in 1944 of the new Education Act, which gave the first definite form and expression to a series of egalitarian and social ideals.

Although the immediate post-war period was drastically affected by shortages, it was from the ferment of this time that new standards of school building developed and fresh approaches to the curriculum began to grow. At first there was a drive to 'get back to normal', meaning a return to the conditions that existed in the days before the war, but this gradually evolved into a general attempt to create a new relationship between the school and the community. It certainly appears that this was the original motivation behind the various efforts that, during the early 1960s, began to be drawn together into something that could properly be called 'design education'. In nearly every case, the pioneering

work was seen as a response to 'changes in society' and the intention was to fit children more adequately for the technological world in which they were going to live.

In 1967 my wife and I prepared two articles for *Design* magazine that set out to review the way design was then being handled in secondary schools. It included a number of quotes from people who were actively engaged in introducing design studies either in schools or colleges of education. Their approaches were different but their motivation – a response to social change – was strikingly similar. It is worth repeating some of the things that they said.

Geoffrey Harrison told us that the then new *Project Technology* was setting out to answer a number of questions:

The great majority of young school-leavers go straight into an industrial job. Is our approach to the teaching of crafts to boys appropriate to the second half of the twentieth century?

Is the role of technology in modern society given its proper weight in any part of the curriculum – whether the teaching of science or history or social sciences? If not, how could a school set about improving the situation?

Do we take enough advantage of the interest of boys and girls, whatever their age, in building things that work, that may be of benefit to society?

Peter Green, who at the time was head of the department of teacher training at Hornsey College of Art, had just written an article for a short-lived magazine called *Design Education*. We decided to quote from it directly:

If art is a form of expression and communication we should study in detail

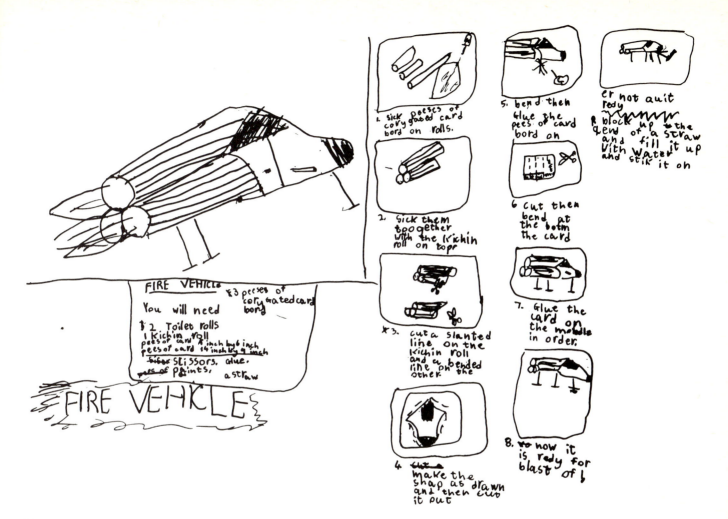

FIRE VEHICLE

You will need

1 2 Toilet rolls
1 Kichin roll
E3 peeces of corrygatedcard bord
pees of card 8 inch by 6 inch
pees of card 14 inch by 9 inch
scissors. glue.
pees of paints, a straw

FIRE VEHICLE

1. sick peeses of corrygated card bord on rolls.

2. sick them toogether with the kichin roll on top

3. cut a slanted line on the kichin roll and a bended line on the other

4. make the shap as drawn and then cut it out

5. bend then glue the pees of card bord on

6 cut then bend at the botm the card

7. Glue the card on the mdle in order.

8. now it is redy for blast of

er not quit redy
block up the end of a straw and fill it up with water and stik it on

Tools

Tom's instruction sheet explaining how to make a model 'fire vehicle', which he designed. The scheme was based on his experience of what could be made using tools and materials with which he was familiar : scissors, glue, sticky tape, cardboard, toilet rolls. The drawing too was a tool : it was not prepared after the vehicle had been constructed as an 'explanation' of what had been done but before, to clarify both the design and the procedures that would be involved in making it.

how in fact ideas can be expressed and concepts communicated.

If design is concerned with the function and appearance of the man-made environment, largely manifest in three dimensions, we should have experience in the widest range of structural and three-dimensional materials and of problems that concern function and appearance.

If our society is dominated by the products of technology, we should begin to study machine processes and the materials of technology – how and why things are made and what exactly is the functional and structural capacity of each particular material.

Such experience in terms of perception, communication, function, structure and appearance may not be limited to drawing and painting. The area of study could include film and television, mathematics and geometry, music and English, light and sound, wood and metalwork and the exploration of the widest possible range of materials . . .

If the nature of a visual, structural or functional problem is studied and clearly defined, and a personal and satisfactory solution arrived at logically and rationally, then the design is achieved through experience – rather than imposed from outside as a doctrine of what is right and acceptable. Such experience in art and design is vitally important for young people. Emphasis must be placed on decision-making exercises in relation to particular problems, analysis of the nature of materials, visual communication and the design process.

We tried to sum up the underlying direction of development in the following way:

There is a continuum of interest emerging which could quite logically link the art room with science and technology without in any way reducing the amount of creative work done in schools. It is not a question of limiting children's imagination by concentrating less on painting and sculpture, but of applying imagination and creativity to broader areas, thus bringing out the essential human basis of applied science as expressed in technology and mass communications.

[At any extreme] interest is more specialised; an engineering based course would not naturally touch on graphics or fashion or film and television, nor would a mass communications based course normally concern itself with bridge building or aeronautics, but the middle ground of engineering and industrial design holds the extremes together and makes linking worth-while. In fact, the interpenetration between technology and culture has now gone so far that some such connexion is long overdue.

In a lecture which I gave to the Architectural Association a few years later I tried to say what, in essence, design education was and was not, why it was worth doing, and what its main potential dangers were. The notes for the talk were as follows:

1 Studying and experiencing design problems at school is not, in the long term, a way of making craftwork palatable, or of making art appear more closely related to everyday 'utilitarian' experience.

2 It is not a way of producing a public who will 'understand' and therefore accept what professionals (planners, architects, designers) provide.

3 It is not primarily a way of turning out adults who have 'good taste'.

Images
*Tom's design for the title for a Batman
and Robin comic.*

So what is it and why do it?

4 Studying and experiencing design is the best possible introduction to the physical and material problems facing twentieth century culture. It brings out the essential interrelationship between, for example, technical and moral questions and between economic and social ones.

5 In a fragmented school curriculum, design is one of a number of subjects that absolutely demand an interdisciplinary treatment. It also provides a number of fresh perspectives on subjects such as geography, history and mathematics, while linking them together. It finds a natural and logical place in a reformed, modern, liberal curriculum.

6 For the individual, it provides good experience in sociology, economics, logic, mathematics, the use of materials, aesthetics, and technology. At its core is the business of weighing priorities and taking decisions about value. It can relate to big general problems and smaller, personal and domestic ones.

7 Most important is that it could lead to a democratisation of the present oligarchic methods of planning and design, gradually giving back to ordinary people more control over the decisions that shape the environment.

What are the main dangers?

8 Framing a course that is supposed to be about design *exclusively* around any of the following:

technology

the study of materials

aesthetics and the cultivation of taste

traditional craftsmanship

free expression

These all play a part, but are more complementary than central: the central element is design activity itself.

9 That design studies themselves become a new orthodoxy, a fixed subject in the curriculum, replete with a complex mechanism of examinations and 'right' answers.

10 That teachers may miss the principal chance offered by design studies, which is a fresh relationship with the pupils. Design studies can never involve 'exercises' the answers to which are known to the teacher and not to the children. There are no known answers in this sense, only answers to be evaluated, with the teacher becoming one of a team of research workers: guiding and leading perhaps, but not dictating.

That identification of the possibilities and problems still appears to me to be accurate, but it would be fair to report that the further development of design education since 1967 has been far from smooth and straightforward. In 1971 I tried to analyse the difficulties in an article that I wrote for *The Times Educational Supplement*. As it was this piece of work that led directly to my involvement in the Royal College of Art research project, and so to the existence of the present book, it is worth quoting from in some detail:

As little as three years ago any article on design education in secondary schools would have had to start with the usual homilies about 'an important but neglected subject'. Today the situation is very different. Pioneering work in Leicestershire, at Cardiff and Hornsey Colleges of Art,

and in Schools Council projects at Loughborough College of Education, Keele University and Goldsmith's College has laid a firm foundation which is now being used as a basis for day-to-day work in schools up and down the country. On 19 June the newly formed Association for Design Education, whose chairman is Bernard Aylward from Leicestershire, is holding a conference at Loughborough to encourage the setting up of local design education groups and, at the end of this summer term, the first candidates will be sitting the new A-level examination in design sponsored by the Oxford Delegacy. Altogether, the picture is one of rapid development that is spreading far beyond the inevitably limited influence of those who originally helped to start it.

The provision of design education at secondary level is now accepted educational policy in quite a large number of places, and is about to be introduced in many others. In some ways, however, this success has made more acute a number of problems of emphasis which were always inherent in design education and which will now have to be resolved. To understand the situation it is necessary to look at the various sources from which design education began. Put very broadly these were as follows:

1 The dissatisfaction of woodwork and metalwork teachers with their subject in its traditional form. Young teachers in this field frequently argued that their basically handicraft methods were irrelevant to the twentieth century, and that their

Utensils
Not exactly a knife or fork but certainly intended to be useful and to extend man's power and his range of possible activities – Tom's design for an amphibious hydroplane.

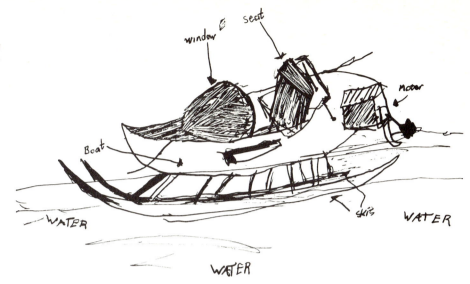

teaching was ineffective as a result. In design they saw a way of giving practical work a new context and of making it important in a society based on mass production

2 The dissatisfaction of art teachers with their subject, particularly in so far as it dealt with rather amorphous notions like 'self expression'. They felt the need of more rational elements, and a closer relationship with the everyday experience of their pupils.

3 The claim that visual education has always been neglected in British schools. This view, supported by many influential individuals and institutions, has at last been acknowledged and has been a powerful influence on the particular way in which design education has been introduced.

4 The development, in education in general, of an understanding of the importance of interdisciplinary work.

This has allowed essentially interdisciplinary subjects, such as design, to be experimented with and welcomed.

5 The desire to make education relevant to industrial society. Here it has been technology that has played the most important part but there has also been a strong influence from the social sciences.

It will quickly be seen that while these five starting points are in no way exclusive, they do lead naturally to varying interpretations of the significance of studying design in schools. Craftsmen emphasise the role of materials, logic and economics; artists the role of feeling and individual insight into otherwise technological processes.

Educationalists often concentrate on the way in which design provides 'windows' on to other subjects, and see it as the key to reorganising such separate areas as art, woodwork, metalwork, technical drawing, and home economics. Social scientists see it most clearly as an aspect of sociology and as a way of giving protection to the consumer-to-be in a capitalist world.

The result is confusion. Or, at least, the lack of any clear vision as to what design education is really about. Paradoxically, the study of design in schools is in danger of being sunk under the various advantages it is supposed to offer! A key point here is that none of the starting points so far described is essentially concerned with the development of design itself, or with the techniques of designing.

Symptomatic of the confusion and the problems it causes is the debate about the 'best age to introduce design work'. Linked with this is a whole network of difficulties about the curriculum and the order in which essential elements should be presented to children. 'Can they design until they understand aesthetics?' 'Can they design without having studied problem solving?' 'Surely they need to understand materials and craftsmanship before they can start to design a chair?' Designing tends to be seen as the distant goal that will only come at the end of a whole lot of other experiences.

To suggest that this 'sequence of experiences' is nothing but the old subjects wrapped up in new packaging would be churlish but, on the other hand, its origins are sometimes rather plain. As, also, is the fact that it betrays a lack of confidence in the nature and complexity of the core activity – design itself.

Even this was not the sum of the difficulties. A special kind of problem arose in those schools where 'integrated' faculties or departments called 'design' or 'creative design' had been organised. Generally, such amalgamations involved art, handicraft and home economics. When the arrangement was first introduced, in Leicestershire in 1967, it is clear that it was intended as a step towards achieving a more ideal human and physical setting for art, design and craft education. The intended flexibility related to the whole concept of 'opportunity' as represented by the comprehensive principle at its best, and the interdisciplinary nature of the resulting faculties reflected, in an exciting way, the nature of design as an exploratory, open-ended, interdisciplinary activity. However, the concept did not always transplant well. Some authorities copied the example without the careful preparation of buildings and staff that characterised the work in Leicestershire. Some even used the reorganisation as a way of cutting back on the total of facilities, staff and time allocated to the subject areas involved.

By the start of the Royal College of Art research project in 1974, this had become a burning issue. The Art Advisers Association had come out against 'design education', largely on the basis of its being identified with the idea of an integrated departmental or faculty structure. Home economics teachers were widely dissatisfied with what they believed to be the distorting effect that the arrangement had on their own educational aims and objectives. Horror stories abounded about the trivialising effects of thematic work in the setting of a 'materials circus'. It was easy to hear of Swiss rolls whose inspiration was supposed to be 'circles' and to see gingerbread bicycles labelled 'movement'.

The tragedy here was the very real possibility that a great educational opportunity was being missed. There was nothing inherent in the idea of combined facilities or a faculty structure that meant that it would lead to trivialisation. In fact, the original intention was the opposite: that it would make it possible to break out of the trivialisation of subject boundaries. The problem was evidently not in the concept but in the management of it.

What was required, at this point, was to distinguish between organisation and content. It needed to be recognised that an integrated faculty might or might not, in practice, turn out to be a good place in which to conduct design education. Whether it was or not would depend in each case entirely on the activities that it contained. It was a structure that offered, and still offers, special potential and possibilities, but it is now clear that design education can also be effectively carried on within other types of school organisation.

During the course of the Royal College of Art research project, we have been concerned to untie the knot that has come to bind together the general concept of 'design studies' with the particular concept of 'design faculties'. Historically, the connexion was logical enough but, by 1974, it was causing acute difficulty and adding to the prevailing atmosphere of doubt and confusion.

Against this background of widespread but mainly incoherent change, how are we to characterise the present state of design education? And how can the present book about design in general be said to relate to it and its future development?

At the philosophical level there is an area of great confusion about terminology, but this only conceals an even greater area of difficulty about understanding the nature of design and its relationship with art, home economics, handicraft, technology and other school subject areas. On the other hand, where interdisciplinary groups of teachers have met and worked together over a relatively long period of time, an area of real agreement about aims and objectives has begun to emerge. The outlines of a 'core' of knowledge, experience and technique are also becoming visible that genuinely could unite the range of specialists involved and form the content of design studies in the future. Something else important is happening wherever long-term discussions have been going on: the similarities between artists, craftsmen, designers, technologists, environmentalists and home makers are beginning to appear to be more important – in the context of general education – than their differences. It is here that a book for teachers about design may hope to make its main contribution. The core of the discussion in Chapters 2, 3, 4 and 6 is directed to that end.

The next point is that there is considerable evidence that a widespread and realistic debate on the value of particular teaching methods is in progress in the schools. The general direction of change is towards a more 'child centred'

approach with the focus of concern moving slowly from 'teaching' to 'learning'. This concept must be of key importance in design studies. It is an approach that accords with a great deal of contemporary liberal thinking in education. The interesting thing is that this kind of work is now moving, step by step, from a theoretical beginning to practical realisation in school situations that are often far from ideal. For the future understanding of design in schools and in the community, this is one of the most significant developments that could take place. Some of the main issues involved are dealt with in Chapters 3, 4, 5 and 6.

When teachers turn to the curriculum they have a sharp awareness of the factors that limit change. The whole range of possible constraints, from the attitude of parents to the lack of facilities, impinge on any plan for the future. The attitude of headmasters and the nature of the examination system are of absolutely crucial importance. I hope that some of the arguments presented here will prove convincing to non-specialists and that, as a result, what is said about design here will be something that headmasters, other teachers, parents and the community at large can understand and respond to. As far as examinations are concerned, there is a discussion in Chapter 4 about the nature of design activity in schools that should help to make clear some of the principles and problems that are likely to be involved.

Behind all this there is the idea of self-help. Teachers today are surprisingly critical of much of the curriculum development work that

has been done in the recent past. They believe that the various projects involved should have co-operated more closely so as to have contributed to a more coherent series of proposals and packages, and they are aware that most approaches of this kind will founder without continuing institutional support. As a result, there is now a great deal of enthusiasm for suggestions that curriculum development should, in future, be more locally based. There exists a conviction that this is work that can – and should – be done by teachers, often in the context of their own school and its immediate problems. I am certain that this is right. But it does mean that future development depends on the willingness of teachers to work towards their own salvation and to provide, for themselves, formative experiences that will carry them forward on the basis of personal confidence. Here I hope that some of the basic arguments about design will prove illuminating and that Chapters 5, 6 and the list of books for further reading will go a little further and provide at least a tentative beginning for some practical experiments.

Conceptions of design vary. This is inevitable. For most children, family background, popular mythology and the mass media will be as important as what the teacher says. So will the place in which they live and their perception of it. The child moves through a designed world absorbing its values. This drawing is part of a pictorial 'map' tracing the journey to school: it was produced as a part of the Front Door project at Pimlico.
(Inner London Education Authority)

Chapter 2

What is design?

How you define design depends on what you are trying to do. A definition of design that would be useful to a designer might not help an historian and could possibly outrage a philosopher. For the teacher, the problem is even more acute. He is likely to come into contact not only with his own conception of what design is, but also with the separate conceptions of each of the children he teaches. These, in turn, will have come from family background, popular mythology and the mass media.

The situation is not helped by the existence of conflicting views within the design professions and between various groups of educationalists.

I have a keen sense of schizophrenia over the issue. The part of me that is a designer seeks a narrow and operational definition; the part of me that is an historian seeks for a definition that will reflect the way in which the word has actually been used during the past; and the part of me that is involved in teaching looks for something which will be broad enough to fit the aspirations of liberal education.

The 'design education' approach is perhaps the simplest to describe. As has already been suggested, the field of enquiry is the whole of material culture. Because most material culture is now produced by design, in the operational sense of the word, it is through this lens that the past is viewed and by which its achievements are labelled. This is much to the point. It is coherent and gives a sense of continuity with the past. But it makes it absolutely essential to preserve also a keen awareness of the uniqueness of events in history and, in particular, to preserve an appreciation of the watershed represented by the Industrial Revolution.

It is appropriate to view the past through our own concerns but not to distort its motives or its methods.

It will help to take an example. Imagine a meeting between a medieval master-mason (really an architect and contractor rolled into one) and a contemporary aeronautical engineer. One designed cathedrals, the other designs the airframes of commercial airliners. It is easy to recognise some of the things that they would have in common: an understanding of structure and the capacity of materials; an insight into ways of organising men and equipment; an ability to get large and difficult jobs completed and functioning within given limitations.

On the other hand, it is also easy to see the gulfs that would separate them. The mason would have worked within the limits imposed by a static technology, but one that he could fully understand and could actually carry out himself if need be. Progress in his world meant progress towards goals and ideals defined in the Christian concept of salvation: the movement of the individual soul towards heaven in the setting of an unchanging social order. His feats of engineering had no general commercial motivation to drive them forward.

In each of these respects the world of the aeronautical engineer is precisely opposite. His whole existence depends upon a technology that actively pursues change, but he does not expect to be able to carry out all its processes himself. He is the heir to a tradition that believes in progress and searches for it through the specific media of science and technology. He may not necessarily believe in God; certainly he is forced to accept that society is embarked upon a period of drastic and unceasing change and that this upheaval is in part the result of the activities of engineers like himself.

The aeronautical engineer is involved in design in the nineteenth century sense, whereas the mason was not. He was, more accurately, a craftsman. But, in the context of design education, we also find ourselves having to use the word to indicate the larger and more embracing fact that both are concerned in the creation of material culture. Both thoughts are essential to an understanding of the evolution of design: we need to be able to think and speak about both of them without too much confusion.

What we have here is the need to distinguish between design used to describe the employment of a particular set of methodologies (bounded by the limits of time and place) and design used as a generic term for all the creative work involved

Continuity or discontinuity? Old and new feats of engineering standing out dramatically from their more humble surroundings: Durham Cathedral and the Severn Bridge. What would their designers have had in common? Certainly an interest in structure and in 'getting things done'. But separating them and their societies would be a gulf in terms of morals and motivation. (Chris Ridley)

in the making of material culture, whatever the methodology and whatever the motive.

A similar clash occurs between design in the limited sense of particular methodologies and design extended to embrace the social, economic and cultural circumstances of creation and use.

As before, an example will help to clarify the issue. When Thomas Newcomen developed the first commercially successful atmospheric steam pumping engine in 1712, he made one of the greatest technological leaps forward that there has ever been. His achievement can be seen in two different perspectives. The story of what he did can be told either as a 'problem solving' adventure involving a series of brilliant design decisions spread over fourteen years of practical development work, or as the outcome of the interaction between certain existing technological resources and changing social and philosophical ideas.

Letter from Thomas Newcomen to his wife. It is dated 1727, fifteen years after he completed the first commercially successful atmospheric steam pumping engine. It tells us a great deal about the cultural and religious background against which this Nonconformist designer worked and reminds us that such factors are important in understanding the content and meaning of design. 'The Lord grant these Considerations may make Impressions upon all our Minds, to his Care I heartily commend you . . . so shall send the Screws & Pulleys by the next Vessell.'
(The Curator of the Dartmouth Museum)

26

The questions asked in the broader of these two contexts are: why did Newcomen do what he did and why was he successful? The theoretical basis for the atmospheric engine that he built appears to have been known to the Romans and some knowledge of it probably existed in medieval times. But science was not greatly interested in the application of knowledge even in the eighteenth century; that development followed rapidly, but only after the Industrial Revolution had already begun. Newcomen's biographer, L T C Rolt,* gave a good description of the scientific background against which he worked:

By founding the Royal Society in 1660, Charles II set the seal of royal patronage and approval upon the new spirit of scientific inquiry and speculation which, in England, as in Europe, was the *zeitgeist* of the Renaissance. Yet this significant ferment of activity was, in Newcomen's day, still almost exclusively confined to the study and the laboratory bench. Knowledge was pursued for its own sake and, although very significant discoveries were made, the discoverers were seldom concerned to apply their knowledge to practical purpose...

Between [a] small and exclusive band of craftsmen [the scientific instrument makers] and the makers of all those practical things by which man seeks to lighten his daily toil an immense gulf was fixed. For example, the makers of wind and watermills built solidly and well, but with such massive crudity and ignorance of principle that it is almost impossible for us to believe that workmanship so medieval in character could be contemporary with that of the great horologists and instrument makers of

seventeenth century London. For many years there was no bridging this gulf. Instrument making was a 'mystery', a jealously guarded closed shop, while the scientists of the day looked upon the practical man, who lived by the skill of hand and eye, with a certain arrogance and contempt that is typified in their attitude towards Thomas Newcomen.

But there were others who did not look on Newcomen with contempt. It was their existence that made a decisive contribution to the success of his enterprise. What is more, it was their *zeitgeist*, the commercial, progress-seeking *zeitgeist* of the coming Industrial Revolution, which also inspired Newcomen as a man and gave him the determination to bring his work to a successful conclusion. Newcomen applied all his great skill as a designer-craftsman to the problems of innovation, but he could not have done it if he had not lived at a time when a sufficient number of men believed innovation to be possible and saw that it could be applied to transform their business and to make a profit.

If we discuss Newcomen simply as a man wrestling with a series of design problems, we wrench him out of the broader cultural and economic background which gives him his essential drama and meaning for posterity. If, on the other hand, we ignore his role as a designer-craftsman, we lose the central element of his character: it makes it appear that innovation in design happens almost automatically as a result of social pressures, and this is simply not true. The activity of designing and the personality of the designer leave their vital stamp on what is produced.

From this clash of definitions it is

now possible to isolate four quite distinct themes that the word design has to be used for, but which need also to retain a separate identity as well as an interrelationship:

1 As a collective concept embracing the creative effort and related ideas and perceptions involved in all material culture, from whatever place and time and for whatever motive.

2 As an exclusive concept defining a particular set of methodologies which developed as a result of the Industrial Revolution.

3 As a collective concept embracing the social and economic influence exerted on and by those methodologies.

4 As a concept within general education (eg 'design education') that indicates the attempt to study formally, by whatever means, the phenomena indicated in 1, 2 and 3.

* 'Thomas Newcomen: the prehistory of the steam engine', L T C Rolt, David and Charles, 1963.

Table 1

A first definition of design and related terms developed by Professor L Bruce Archer as a part of the Royal College of Art 'Design in General Education' project.

It is interesting to relate these themes to the working definitions developed by Professor Archer and adopted in the study at the Royal College of Art. They are given in detail in Table 1. It is likely that these will be modified further, but it is significant that the parallels are very close. Similar thematic matrices have been suggested in relation to other subject areas in the school curriculum. Structurally an approach of this kind is essential if multidisciplinary chaos is to be avoided. It seems likely that, in the future, the RCA terminology will be adopted by the design professions and by educationalists. The emergence of agreed definitions is of cardinal importance in the evolution of any discipline. It also indicates the breadth of responsibility and cultural involvement that are now foreseen by designers.

But for practising teachers all such structures have a weakness in common: they lack human warmth and concrete immediacy. They do not have the bite and poignancy of the real surroundings that men inhabit and the actual tools and utensils that they use. It is these, in all their marvellous diversity, that are the practical flesh on the theoretical skeleton that we have just examined.

1 **DESIGN** is the area of human experience, skill and knowledge that reflects man's concern with the appreciation and adaptation of his surroundings in the light of his material and spiritual needs. In particular, it relates with configuration, composition, meaning, value and purpose in man-made phenomena
(Analogous with Humanities, Science)

Hence:

2 **DESIGN AWARENESS** is design as philosophy. It is consciousness of configuration, composition, meaning, value and purpose in man-made phenomena and the ability to understand and handle ideas related with them
(Analogous with literacy and numeracy)

3 **DESIGN ACTIVITY** is design as an art. It is the set of skills by which man adapts things to suit him better
(Analogous with technology, skill)

4 **DESIGN EDUCATION** is the mechanism effecting the transmission of the body of ideas, information and technique which constitutes the received state of knowledge and skill. It may be concerned primarily with design awareness or it may be concerned primarily with design activity. Most often it will contain some of both

Further sub-divisions are possible, for example, under design awareness:

5 **DESIGN SENSIBILITY**, which is the development of the ability to discriminate different kinds and degrees of configuration, order, value, purpose and meaning

6 **DESIGN HISTORY**, which like natural history, represents not only the study of design phenomena in the past, but also a systematic account of how things come to be the way they are

Under design activity:

7 **DESIGN SCIENCE**, which is the body of knowledge that is significant for the understanding of design phenomena and for the pursuit of design activity

8 **DESIGN CRAFT**, which is the skill and technique that is significant for the handling of design phenomena and for the exercise of design activity

And under design education:

9 **DESIGN STUDIES**, which are specific learning experiences related with design awareness or design activity

10 **DESIGN RESEARCH**, which is systematic enquiry calculated to produce knowledge significant for design awareness or design activity

Table 2
Definitions
of design

From **DESIGN METHODS** by J C Jones

Finding the right physical components of a physical structure
(Alexander, 1963)

A goal-directed problem-solving activity
(Archer, 1965)

Decision making, in the face of uncertainty, with high penalties for error
(Asimow, 1962)

Simulating what we want to make (or do) before we make (or do) it as many times as may be necessary to feel confident in the final result
(Booker, 1964)

The conditioning factor for those parts of the product which come into contact with people
(Farr, 1966)

Engineering design is the use of scientific principles, technical information and imagination in the definition of a mechanical structure, machine or system to perform prespecified functions with the maximum economy and efficiency
(Feilden, 1963)

Relating product with situation to give satisfaction
(Gregory, 1966)

The performing of a very complicated act of faith
(Jones, 1966)

The optimum solution to the sum of the true needs of a particular set of circumstances
(Matchett, 1968)

The imaginative jump from present facts to future possibilities
(Page 1966)

A creative activity – it involves bringing into being something new and useful that has not existed previously
(Reswick, 1965)

To initiate change in man-made things
(Jones, 1970)

From **DESIGN IN CRAFT EDUCATION**
by the Association of Advisors in Design and Technical Studies

DESIGN is:
Noun
Mental plan; scheme of attack;
purpose; end in view; adaptation
of means to end; preliminary
sketch for a picture; delineation,
pattern; artistic or literary
groundwork, general idea,
construction, plot, faculty of
evolving these, invention

Verb
Set (thing) apart for person;
destine (person, thing) for a
service; contrive, plan; intend;
make preliminary sketch of
(picture); draw plan of (building
etc to be executed by others); be a
designer; conceive mental plan of,
(book, work of art).
*(Extracted and slightly edited from
the Concise Oxford Dictionary)*

The antithesis of accident
(Vernon Barber)

VISUAL DESIGN
is concerned with images whose
function is to communicate and
inform visually; signs, symbols, the
meaning of forms and colours and
the relations between these

INDUSTRIAL DESIGN
is concerned with functional
objects, designed according to
economic facts and the study of
technique and materials

GRAPHIC DESIGN
works in the world of the Press, of
books, of printed advertisements,
and everywhere the printed word
appears, whether on a sheet of
paper or a bottle

RESEARCH DESIGN
is concerned with experiments of
both plastic and visual structures in
two or more dimensions. It tries
out the possibilities of combining
two or more dimensions, attempts
to clarify images and methods in
the technological field, and carries
out research into images on film
*(From Design as Art by Bruno
Munari – Pelican 1972)*

ENGINEERING DESIGN
is the use of scientific principles,
technical information and
imagination in the definition of a
mechanical structure, machine or
system to perform prespecified
functions with the maximum
economy and efficiency
(From Feilden Report 1963)

DESIGNERS
Every human being is a designer.
Many also earn their living by
design – in every field that warrants
pause and careful consideration
between the conceiving of an
action, a fashioning of the means to
carry it out, and an estimation of
its effects
*(From Design as Art by Bruno
Munari – Pelican 1972)*

A new kind of artist, a creator
capable of understanding every
kind of need: not because he is a
prodigy, but because he knows how
to approach human needs
according to a precise method
(Walter Gropius 1919)

Table 3
Definitions
of design

As a human expression, design defies brief description. The interweaving of themes possible from even the simple four-part matrix given above provides a slippery reality. Words cannot easily hold it; they can easily distort it. The difficulty is demonstrated as soon as a number of definitions of design are placed side by side as they are on the previous pages. Although some of the suggestions are full of insight, and nearly all are effective in making us look again at our own attitudes and preconceptions, each, in turn, is inadequate by itself. The problem is fundamental. Such simple, coherent definitions distort by the very fact of being simple and coherent. Design is not to be caught in this way. It is inevitable that there is no single definition in the list that truly satisfies our sense of the reality of design as a quality or activity existing in the real world.

How is the teacher to approach this problem of definition? Does it mean that all the definitions are quite useless? In what way can all this effort at simplification actually help to clarify the nature of design?

It is much more encouraging if we take all the definitions and begin to play them off against each other. Even though some of them appear to contradict, the result is immediately more convincing. The definitions begin to spark one another off, they reveal one another's inadequacies, they illuminate one another, they create a dialectic within which we can explore, accept, reject, and perhaps eventually understand. At once we are nearer to having enough voices and attitudes to go round. This variety is the point and we really need it. Look at any land or townscape in Britain.

What you see is entirely the creation of men working with the materials that the land has supplied. Every piece of it is the result of human decisions. With such a scene in view it is easy to understand why it is an impossibly trivial undertaking to attempt to encompass in a single sentence a useful collective description for such a vast mass of thought, work, sensibility and economic calculation.

In a book on the relationship between art and society,* I wrote that 'The material gathered in the world's great museums is only the tip of a colossal iceberg, the base of which stretches away below the surface of the limited range of attitudes and activities that are thought of as "cultural". When the base as well as the top of the structure is included it becomes clear that people's response to life, even their actual experience of it, has always been in all manner of ways determined, described and enlarged by art . . . In looking at the humble and everyday ways in which imagery is applied to life it becomes clear that art is involved in every side of men's activities, positive and negative. It is as truthful as men are truthful; as cynical as men are cynical; as frightened or as brave.' This analysis applies with even greater force to material culture as a whole. It is a receptacle and a mould for every aspect of human activity.

The most lasting impression left by a visit to a none-too-discriminating junk shop or an 'unreformed' provincial folk museum is of a treasure trove of human ephemera. Somewhere, in the contents of a thousand such collections, could be found sufficiently diverse material for a popular history of design, or rather for a history of design as most people who were not wealthy patrons really experienced it. There exists a vivid, though fictional, picture of the kind of muddle I am thinking of. It is a description of the room occupied by Merlin the magician in *The Once and Future King*.† To understand the variety of his possessions it is necessary to know that Merlin was living backwards through time. He owned things from his past which, in the medieval romance period when he was supposed to be alive, were in other people's distant future. Thus he was able to make a personal world from the design resources of many centuries and mythologies.

It was the most marvellous room he had ever been in. There was a real corkindrill hanging from the rafters, very lifelike and horrible with glass eyes and scaly tail stretched out behind it. When its master came into the room it winked one eye in salutation although it was stuffed. There were thousands of brown books in leather bindings some chained to the bookshelves and others propped against each other as if they had had too much to drink, and they did not really trust themselves. These gave out a smell of must and solid brownness which was most secure. Then there were stuffed birds, popinjays, and maggot-pies, and kingfishers and peacocks with all their feathers but two, and tiny birds like beetles, and a reputed phoenix which smelt of incense and cinnamon . . .

There was a guncase with all sorts of weapons which would not be invented for half a thousand years, a rod-box ditto, a chest of drawers full of salmon flies which had been tied by Merlin himself, another chest whose drawers were labelled Mandrogora, Mandrake, Old Man's Beard etc, a bunch of turkey feathers and goosequills for making pens, an astrolabe, twelve pairs of boots, a dozen purse-nets, three dozen rabbit wires, twelve corkscrews, some ants' nests between two glass plates, ink-bottles of every possible colour from red to violet, darning-needles, a gold medal for being the best scholar at Winchester, four or five recorders, a nest of field mice all alive-o, two skulls, plenty

Right
'*Look at any land or townscape in Britain: what you see is entirely the creation of men working with the materials that the land has supplied.*' *This aerial view of Battersea shows the remains of an old pattern of roads and eighteenth century building around Clapham Common (centre top). During the Industrial Revolution the railways were built across what was then largely open country covered by market gardens serving London. In the subsequent eras of expansion, thousands of small houses, together with shops, schools and churches to serve them, spread to fill in the spaces and a new shopping centre was created beside Clapham Junction station. The impetus to clear slums and create a new London is represented both by early industrial tenements and modern GLC housing, which break up the pattern of small streets. The complex structure of the city reflects the complex mixture of motives and resources that went into it. (Aerofilms Limited)*

* 'Art in Society', Ken Baynes, Lund Humphries, 1975.

† 'The Once and Future King', T H White, Collins, 1958.

Design reflects every side of man's character. This series of photographs by Peter Jones demonstrates just a few of the motives that may result in the construction of buildings or the manufacture of products.

Top left
The desire to apply mechanical power to difficult work. A Cornish pumping engine.

Top right
The need to symbolise life's great and terrible events. War memorial.

Right
The feeling for pattern and order. Market stall.

The need for personal adornment. A rocker's jacket.

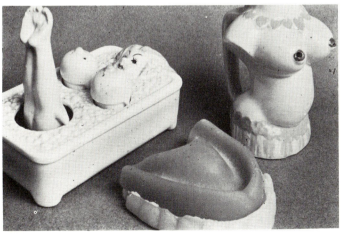

The fun of a good laugh. Seaside souvenirs.

of varnish, some satsuma china, and some cloisonné, the fourteenth edition of the Encyclopaedia Britannica (marred as it was by the sensationalism of the popular plates), two paint boxes (one oil, one water colour), three globes of the known geographical world, a few fossils, the stuffed head of a cameleopard, six pissmires, some glass retorts with cauldrons, bunsen burners etc., and a complete set of cigarette cards depicting wild fowl by Peter Scott.

The magician's pot-pourri of man-made bric-à-brac is extreme, but it is easy enough to recognise in it a personal detail torn from the incredibly more vast canvas of society as a whole.

I want to give at least one glimpse of a somewhat larger picture than this because the presentation of such a picture is a key aim for design education. The problem is to find ways of seeing, analysing and interpreting that open out from landscapes, buildings and artefacts into the variety of the lives and ideas that produced them. Here, in an extended extract from W G Hoskins's book *The Making of the English Landscape,** is the story of the view from his study window:

The view from this room where I write . . . is small, but it will serve as an epitome of the gentle unravished English landscape. Circumscribed as it is, with tall trees closing it in barely half a mile away, it contains in its detail something of every age from the Saxon to the nineteenth century. A house has stood on this site since the year 1216, when the Bishop of Lincoln ordained a vicarage here, but it has been rebuilt over and over again, and last of all in 1856. Down the garden,

* '*The Making of the English Landscape*', W G Hoskins, Hodder and Stoughton, *1955*.

sloping to the river, the aged and useless apple trees are the successors of those that grew here in the time of Charles I, when the glebe terrier of 1634 speaks of 'one orchard, one backside, and two little gardens'. Beyond the apple trees and within a few feet of the river is a large raised platform, visible in winter before its annual submergence in weeds, part of a vanished building, and there are clear lines of stone walls adjoining it. Almost certainly this is the site of one of the three water-mills recorded on the estate in the Domesday Book. Below it flows the Dorn, known to the Saxons as the Milk, from the cloudiness of its water after rain: and one still sees it as the Saxons saw it a thousand years ago, as I saw it a few minutes ago in the rain drifting down from the Cotswolds.

Across the stream, tumbling fast on its way to Glyme and Evenlode, one sees a wide sedgy hollow planted with willow saplings, from which flocks of goldfinches rise with a flash of wings on sunny mornings. This hollow, enclosed by a massive earthen bank, was the fishpond begun by the lord of the manor before his death in 1175, and completed by his son: 'Ode de Berton grants to Roger de St John the land between the garden of Roger and the road to the bridge together with the moor where Thomas de St John began to make his fishpond, rendering yearly a pair of spurs or twopence'.

This was about the year 1200 (the charter is undated) but there is the fishpond today. And there is the lane dropping down to the stone bridge that was rebuilt in 1948, but unquestionably on the site of the stone bridge which is mentioned as a landmark in an even earlier charter. And 'the moor' is the description of the scene before it had been claimed for cultivation. We catch a sight of an earlier world in the bare words of this charter.

Beyond the fishpond, the ground rises to form the other side of the valley, fields with their broken hedges of twisted

hawthorn. What age are these hedges? They were not here in 1685, when another glebe terrier shows that the parish still had its open fields. But they were probably made before 1750, by which date the enclosure had apparently been accomplished. One or two hedgebanks are, however, medieval in origin, for the St Johns had a separate enclosed pasture called Grascroft from the early 1200s onwards, and this ancient field comes into the view also.

A little to the right, on the other side of the lane, the eye dwells upon a small park, with a boating-lake catching the light, and some modest landscaping; and through the bare winter trees one sees the chimneys of a seemly Victorian 'big

house'. The house and park were made as late as the 1870s. It must be one of the last parks to be made in England, for landowners began to feel the pinch of falling rents soon after that. The house, in fact, is older, for the work of the 1870s though apparently a complete rebuilding, is merely a stone casing around a house originally built by a successful merchant of the Staple, whose inscription is still over the door: 'Thinke and Thanke Anno 1570'. Three hundred years later this house was remodelled by another successful bourgeois – this time a wealthy Oxford brewer.

But this was an old, long-cultivated estate when John Dormer the merchant stapler acquired it, with a history

'The treasure trove of human ephemera.'
These pieces of equipment from a
nineteenth century doll's house are
miniature versions of the extraordinary
variety of artefacts created and used by
people in their day-to-day existence.
The examples shown are from the
Playthings Past Museum, Rednal.
(Gerald Pates, Gloucester)

stretching back to pre-Conquest days, when it was one of the demesne-farms of the Anglo Saxon kings. When they hunted in Woodstock Park, five miles away, in the tenth and eleventh centuries, they called upon the produce of this large estate (about seven thousand acres then) to feed their household; and one can walk, after the morning's writing, along the broad green lane that was first made to connect the estate with the hunting-park. It was a royal estate in Saxon times, but how far back into that age? What was it when the Saxons captured Eynsham, not many miles away, in the year 571? We do not yet know, but here in this room one is reaching back, in a view embracing a few hundred acres at the most, through ten centuries of English life, and discerning shadowy depths beyond that again.

1

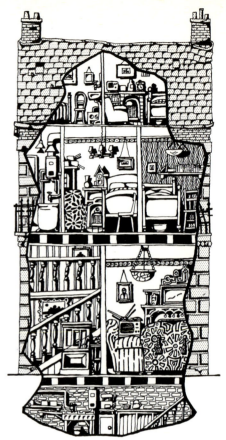

2

'The treasure trove of human ephemera.' In these drawings of three typical houses in an imaginary street, Gerald Nason has brought out the individuality of the interiors. He has written notes on each of the three families.

No 1 The Adamsons, John 35, and Vanessa 32. John is an architect who inherited his father's practice, a good one (moneywise) in a country town. This John disposed of, to move to London. He bought No 1 for £6,500 in 1964 but somehow now he regrets it. In an initial flush of enthusiasm two dividing walls were removed on the first and second floors to make open-plan rooms. The false ceilings in the ground-floor rooms were existent, also the heating plant installed sometime in

the late 1920s. John's study on the ground floor contains mostly furniture from his father's office, kept for sentimental reasons more than anything, since the desk is c. 1951 and the filing cabinet difficult to date. The wallpaper was there and the ceiling light, the latter being what John calls 'an amusing piece of jazz-modern nonsense'. He doesn't know why he kept the wallpaper. The kitchen John and Vanessa had panelled in Swedish style, by a local handyman; John himself

designed the mysterious cooker cupboard. Furniture in the living room was bought for the previous house and, although pleasant enough, begins to look dated (at least in Vanessa's eyes). John's pride and joy is the bedroom, a combination of cheap second-hand chests of drawers, scraped and waxed, and his own hand-made bed and shelves. This has been described by one of John's more successful friends as Neo-Brutalist, as John's handling of materials always was pretty basic. John

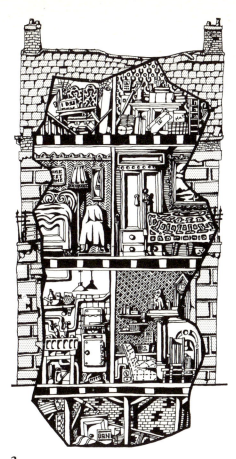

3

works now in the office of a successful firm of property developer's architects. His job isn't a very important one, but it carries a pension and Vanessa would still like children.

No 2 Mrs Panowski, 53. Nobody really knows how June Panowski acquired No 2 as she moved in in that muddled time around 1946. Separated from her husband (a free-Polish pilot attached to the RAF during World War II) she has since rented rooms out to a part of the shifting bed-sit population of London. She herself lives on the first floor (with her kitchen in the basement) and lives now for the 'telly' and her son of 17 who is sometimes in the house, sometimes not. She has picked up her furniture in second-hand shops, consequently it is an ordinary enough mixture of late-Victorian and early post-war. Apart from sub-dividing the first floor, Mrs Panowski has made no changes and since property prices continue to rise she is not unduly worried about the condition of No 2. After all she is only a landlady who one day might retire to a bungalow at Frinton-on-Sea.

No 3 The Hammonds, Jack 76 and Nelly 70. The family left ages ago, but Nelly keeps the first-floor bedroom ready in case Fred ever pops in. Fred is their son, a merchant sailor, who comes home from time to time. He papered the ground-floor living room and put up the contemporary shelves. The other children, all married, have had their pick of the furniture, leaving Jack and Nelly only their favourite pieces; the bedstead and the wardrobe principally, which they bought as newly-weds. The kitchen is a terrible trial to Nelly; somehow Fred never does anything to that, while the second-floor rooms contain only memories of the family and one day will surprise everybody with their worth. Jack has always lived in London, but Nelly was a country girl so she keeps reminding him that, although there must always be a home for Fred, they could retire to Sussex. If they ever sell the house they will.

A similar story could be told about a city street or a country market place. Historical change, economic development, traditions of thought and craftsmanship, social and political expectations; these are the stuff that underpin the structure of the world we see.

The kind of diversity that we have been discussing in all this comes fundamentally from the very great variety of needs, attitudes and interests that exist in the community. It is this variety that defies neat categorisation and destroys the universality of definitions of design. The diversity reflects the varied nature of the people who use the buildings and things that designers design. And, of course, designers are diverse as well. They are not automata without feelings or foibles. Some are serious; some are humorous. Some are given to flights of fancy; some to the most dour preoccupation with unremitting practicality. Some work from an insight into and respect for materials; some see a material as a servant to do as it is told. Some respect tradition; others despise it.

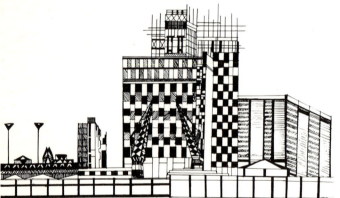

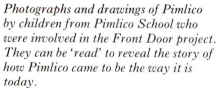

Photographs and drawings of Pimlico by children from Pimlico School who were involved in the Front Door project. They can be 'read' to reveal the story of how Pimlico came to be the way it is today.
(Inner London Education Authority)

It is significant that the majority of the definitions of design quoted earlier were originally written by designers in an attempt to understand and codify their own activities. They are distillations of experience, made to clarify and direct future practice. In that sense they are pieces of history; they are a part of the phenomenon which they are attempting to define. They tell us what design meant to *that* man who worked and wrote at *that* time, who had been educated in a particular way and who saw himself as the heir to *this* or *that* tradition or method of working.

The point is that design is a historically determined activity, evolving as societies evolve, always trapped by the nature of its starting point, but always developing and transforming itself in sympathy with the community it serves. It is something that exists in all societies, but differently in each. To understand this aspect of its role in the world, the need is not to devise a single, watertight, all-purpose definition but instead to develop an eye for its richness, an awareness of the many guises it has adopted, and an appreciation of the various human needs that it has served. It is useful to know as many definitions as possible because, at various times, men have emphasised the most contradictory virtues and vices in the societies, buildings and products that they have created. In the future we may need this awareness if we ever want to break with the particular circumstances in which design now operates. For design, diversity has an evolutionary potential.

What is the nature of design today? What are its characteristic values and

procedures? To work towards an answer to these questions means returning to the watershed of the Industrial Revolution. It was at this point that design began to evolve most clearly out of craftsmanship and to differentiate itself as 'a particular set of methodologies'. It is here that we can find the roots of what has become the modern world's way of creating its most characteristic types of buildings and products.

Perhaps more than any other single thing, the discoveries of science made possible the Industrial Revolution and, therefore, the highly complex urban surroundings and 'man-made' countryside in which most of us now live. All through this book we will find that we are talking about problems, possibilities and activities that could not have existed without the empirical and fact-testing experience of science. However, it is important to realise that science, of itself, need not have had a decisive effect on the everyday world. As has already been suggested in the Newcomen example, there had also to exist the economic, social and craft conditions that would allow the theoretical knowledge inherent in science to find a practical application.

The story has often been told of how the social and economic strands of what was to be the Industrial Revolution gradually evolved from medieval times. Marx, writing in the middle of the nineteenth century, saw in this development a movement towards a higher and more subtle form of society – capitalism – that

Opposite
The first goods shed at Bristol, from a lithograph by the famous railway topographer J C Bourne. (Cambridge University Library)

Above
Workmen travelling to work: the London Underground in the days of steam. An engraving by Gustav Doré.

Design, in the modern sense, is the result of the Industrial Revolution. Cotton spinning was the first industry to be mechanised but it was the development of railways that played a key part socially, economically and technically. The railways demanded on the one hand new capital industries while, on the other, they made industry and large cities possible by moving people and goods.

would in turn give way to an even higher form – communism. The exponents of the new economic theories of the eighteenth century saw the passing of feudalism as an unmitigated blessing and hailed the emergence of large-scale trade and industry as the dawn of the first era of widespread wealth. They claimed that it would be as different from the backward past as a mud hut was from a palace. It has certainly proved to be different. Modern social historians recognise the growth of medieval commerce and the emergence of new philosophies and social attitudes in the Renaissance as essential first steps in a continuum of change that built up, through the Reformation and the eighteenth century 'enlightenment', to an irrepressible industrial and political explosion in the years immediately before the French Revolution.

The technical part of the story is far less well documented and researched. It seems certain that technique changed in a far less consistent way. At the start, it is probable that hardly any novel methods were involved; they were drawn from the repertoire of existing craft skills and knowledge that reached back from the eighteenth century to before the Renaissance. It was ideology, the idea of 'progress', that affected both science and craftsmanship – but separately. In the initial stages we may guess that the decisive thing was to see the commercial potential of the techniques that were already in existence.

It was directly out of the meeting between craftsmanship and commerce that modern engineering was born. But it was when science was added to engineering – as quickly happened – that the practical basis was laid for the mechanics of the nineteenth century, and the start of the process that led eventually to mass production and automation.

The vital and immediate change that engineering made possible was in the means of distribution. The invention of the steam engine was a climactic event because the industrial demand that the railways created was a sound basis on which to develop further capital industries. But the railways also supported other social and economic changes and their arrival decisively marked the end of the old and stable rural society. The railways did more than support industry and distribute its products; they made industrial cities possible by supplying them with vital perishable foods and carrying large numbers of people to and from work.

Engineering was also the key to the development of mass production that, by faltering steps, has gradually led to millions of people having the opportunity to own complex pieces of machinery. Mass production, with all its revolutionary consequences for individuals in society, is probably the most important single element in the events that have transformed everyday life in the last 150 years. Its techniques call for a carefully worked out and rigid plan of manufacture so that each aspect of a particular piece of work can be specialised. The manufacturer has to produce something that can be sold in large quantities to people he cannot meet in person. All this is quite different from what was the craftsman's method of working. The craftsman frequently knew the people who would eventually use what he had made and, if he did not, at least he had a clear conception of their lives and tastes. He also had very complete control over the production of what he 'designed', and often made it entirely with his own hands. The first impact of mass production was on the making of consumer goods in factories, but something of the same kind eventually came to affect every aspect of production and construction. Mass production was something quite new when applied on a vast scale and it toppled the slowly developed traditions of centuries.

It is hardly surprising that the new techniques were not always well understood, or that the older handworking methods were gradually debased. The process took a long time – much Victorian work was of high quality and used excellent materials – but the collapse of tradition was inexorable. Men sometimes used machines to produce shoddy goods for the domestic market and the bad effects of this were compounded because mass production inevitably meant that many people were employed in dull, repetitive jobs. People were metaphorically swallowed alive by their machines.

A broadly based philosophical change interacted with science and engineering to bring about profound alterations in the structure of society. One of the great driving forces since the later part of the eighteenth century has been the desire of the mass of people for political justice and a share in higher material living standards. This is a revolution that is still in progress, now accelerated and sharpened in urgency by the partial success that has already been

CRYSTAL ✦ PALACE ✦ COMPANY

WATT
STEPHENSON
BRUNEL

GALVANI
FARADAY
VOLTA

ROGER BACON

RAPHAEL

INTERNATIONAL
ELECTRIC EXHIBITION
1882.
This is to Certify
that the Jurors have awarded a
GOLD MEDAL
TO
RANSOMES, HEAD & JEFFERIES
FOR STEAM ENGINES.

Secretary   *Chairman*

The Victorians believed in progress, science and engineering. They were confident of their ability to transform the world for the better by means of technology. Significantly, the names of the great designers of the period – Watt, Stephenson, Brunel – appear on this certificate beside those of Raphael and Roger Bacon. (Museum of English Rural Life, University of Reading)

achieved and by the new awareness that our natural resources are finite. Ideas of equality have a long history, but it was not until the Industrial Revolution that equality in material terms became a practical possibility.

Seen in isolation, the Industrial Revolution and the effects it had on society can appear as a terrible episode, a period in which hypocrisy and greed were institutionalised as the respectable aims of the state and the individual. In comparison with the eighteenth century, the Victorian age appears stained and ugly, overblown in some aspects, poverty-stricken in others. But in many ways this is a superficial judgement on a period that saw the birth of the modern conscience and modern social responsibility. The Victorians had to cope with an entirely unprecedented situation, and if they built heartless slums and sometimes exploited human misery and ignorance, they also created a universal system of primary education, reformed the corruption that had crippled local government in the eighteenth century, and set us on the road to the great experiment of the welfare state.

Looking today at the worn-out cities that the Industrial Revolution produced – cities built on greed and real suffering – it is easy enough to grasp the negative side of the nineteenth century. But a really positive change was there, embodied in mass education and the progressive distribution of wealth on a wider basis. Gradually, for the first time in history, the wider experience of life and culture that had always been the preserve of the leisured minority was becoming available to the mass of people. One of the most profound

results of this tremendous change from aristocratic to mass society is that patronage is now broadly based, to be used either by individuals to satisfy their own needs or collectively through societies, companies, and government agencies. Although the success and extension of the egalitarian ideal is not something of which we are particularly conscious, our environment, our entertainment, many of our problems, and most of our new institutions reflect it and are a result of it.

These three themes – science, engineering as expressed in modern methods of distribution and mass production, and the shift of patronage from the few to the many in an egalitarian society – form the background against which the contemporary idea of design has come into being. It is impossible to talk about modern design without taking them into consideration. Design is the direct result of specialisation in industry. Industry is the essential prop of mass society. Modern industry would be impossible without a good distribution system dependent on engineering. And none of these things could exist without science. In the setting of this broad range of interacting changes, there were also much more specific alterations in industrial organisation that pointed directly to the development of a skill called 'designing' and the emergence of a person called a 'designer'.

The immediate cause of this development was specialisation in industry. Long before the process was named, there were people who carried out the designer's function. As soon as the old craft methods were sufficiently broken up, a designer

became a necessity. He took over one particular aspect of the activity that the craftsman had been able to encompass by himself or with only a few close associates.

In a book* that he wrote for children some years ago, Sir Gordon Russell gave a vivid picture of this process of specialisation in the furniture industry. He outlined the work of a country furniture maker just before the Industrial Revolution, describing each step in the process of making and selling chairs and giving, in brackets, the name of the specialist who would carry out the same function in the industry today:

Bill Battersby used to go to a nearby coppice where he knew good straight ash-poles were growing. He selected a number, marked them with white paint, and bought them standing from the farmer who owned the coppice. Today he would have been called a Timber Merchant. Then with his son he cut them down (Timber Feller), and carted them to his workshop (Haulier). Arrived there, he split some up with wedges and sawed others in a saw-pit (Sawyer). He then stacked some to season (Labourer), and others he turned while green (Turner) to designs which he had evolved by trial and error over a long period (Industrial Designer). He then assembled the parts (Chairmaker), and rushed the seats (Upholsterer). Finally, he stained and polished them (Polisher).

He then loaded them on a cart (Packer), and took them to the nearest town (Carter). Arrived there, he set up a stall in the market place (Advertiser), and set them out (Shopkeeper). He sold them (Salesman) and received the money (Cashier). He then went to the Red Lion for a well-earned pot of beer. In the bar he

* *'The Story of Furniture'* (Puffin), Sir Gordon Russell, Penguin Books, 1947.

met his customers in a friendly way and listened to their approval or complaints (Public Relations Officer and Market Research Group). Finally, he went home with various orders in his head or on old slips of paper (Traveller). These he put in a teapot on the mantel-shelf, to be taken out as required (Book-keeper).

The same process could be paralleled in practically every industry that has developed from a craft basis and, in new industries like car-making, the degree of specialisation is even greater. The new system of production automatically called for somebody to carry on the creative and formative aspect of the craftsman's work and so a designer was needed.

At this point it is useful to make a distinction historically between the role of the designer on the one hand and the attitudes taken up by those people who self-consciously called themselves designers on the other. In any system of mass production, a designer is required for every building or product that is made, but the majority of people who filled the role were not called designers and did not think of themselves as such. Most design work has always been done by anonymous men in the drawing offices of companies and government departments. We might say that, largely unaffected by the many debates about 'good' and 'bad' design, it is these people who have in practice produced the everyday environment of the majority of people. On the other hand, it is important to understand something of the ideological debate about the role of the designer because it is from this that many of our present ideas about design have developed.

When we come to look at the birth and development of 'modern' design as a coherent concept, we can see that it started as a reaction against the squalor and ugliness that nineteenth century industry was believed to have created. It was part of the larger movement – still going on – to realise to the full the capacity for good industrialisation. As long ago as 1907, in his inaugural address to the first annual meeting of the Deutsche Werkbund, Theodor Fischer outlined the driving forces behind the new movement:

There is no fixed boundary line between tool and machine. Work of a high standard can be created with tools or with machines as soon as man has mastered the machine and made it a tool . . . It is not the machines themselves that make work inferior, but our inability to use them properly . . . It is not mass production and subdivision of labour that are fatal but the fact that industry has lost sight of its aim of producing work of the highest quality, and does not feel itself to be a serving member of our community but the ruler of the age.

This was the essential first step. The machine's potential as a vital and constructive part of culture had to be accepted before the characteristic philosophy of the modern movement could be developed. The starting point, which can be found at the turn of the century, was the bold claim that the new means of production were not an aesthetic curse that would destroy culture, but the basis of a different kind of civilisation that was, in itself, worth-while and exciting. William Morris, speaking for the visually aware people of an earlier generation, had said that 'Art will die out of civilisation, if the system lasts. That in

itself does to me carry with it the condemnation of the whole system.' However, Frank Lloyd Wright, the great American pioneer of modern architecture, turned the tables on the artists and accused them of helping in the machine's degradation by clinging to their own fixed aesthetic standards in the face of the immense potential inherent in the process of industrialisation.

Many of the most interesting aspects of the modern movement were embodied in its attempt to bridge the apparent chasm between art and industry. To do this the pioneers developed a specifically technological approach to the problems of design and elucidated stylistic questions by invoking a morality of humane utilitarianism. In the process, they came to believe not only that there *should* be a uniquely twentieth century vision but also that it was they, and nobody else, who had created it.

20-21

Pavillonfchule · Pavilion school · École à pavillons Frankfurt-Praunheim. Architekt Kaufmann,
ler Pullmann. Schaukälten im Treppenhaus und Schulterralle im Obergefchoß · Show cases on h
and school terrace on the upper storey · Vitrines au cage d'escalier et terrasse d'école à l'e
périeur · Foto Collifchonn

„Nicht die Schulen find moderne Schulen, die, im letzten Jahrzehnt
um ein altes Programm einen neuzeitlichen Mantel hängen, fonder
die dem Grundwefen unferer lebendigen Architekturbewegung gem
geiftige Problem der neuen Schule zum Ausgangspunkt einer neue
ftaltung machen[6]).

[1]) Stadtbaurat Wagner, Berlin, Vom Schulbau unferer Zeit. In: Das Schulhau
    11/12, Seite 246
[2]) Vergl. Karlen-Taut, Die Dammwegfchule Neukölln. Comenius-Verlag, Berlin
[3]) Kade-Kaufmann, Die neue Dorffchule, 1. Heft der „Beiträge zur Landlich
    Herausgeber Kade. Verlag Diefterweg, Frankfurt a. M., 1930
[4]) Schulbauforderungen. Erarbeitet von der Gefellfchaft der Freunde des vaterlär
    Schul- und Erziehungswelens. Hamburg, 1929
[5]) Das neue Schulhaus, Vorfchläge zur baulichen Geftaltung und inneren Aus
    Verlag Die Leipziger Lehrerzeitung, Leipzig 1930
[6]) Das neue Schulhaus, a.a.O., Seite 7
[7]) Vergl. Kerlchenfteiner, Das Problem der Lebensnähe. In: Die Erziehung, 1930,
[8]) May, Die Architektur der neuen Schule. In: Das Schulhaus, 1929, 3 4, Seite 53

Above

It was a characteristic of the modern movement in design to accept the machine as an essential element in life. Its protagonists accepted industrial methods and saw that they might be used to produce works of art and design unique to the twentieth century. They believed that they had the ability to create 'the environment which people needed in order to live an ordered, agreeable and progressive existence in a technological world'. These directions of thought are symbolised by the cover and pages shown here from the German magazine 'Das Neue Frankfurt', which dealt with important design and planning problems during the late 1920s. (Ken and Kate Baynes)

25
PAVILLONSCHULE IN FRANKFURT-BORNHEIM
Pavilion School at Bornheim, Frankfort · Ecole à
pavillons à Francfort-Bornheim · Architekt Ernst
May, Mitarbeiter Albert Loecher. 1930 · Foto Dr.
Wolff. cf. die Publikation in Heft 9, 1930

...fle in den Frankfurter Schulen · Open
...the Francfort Schools · Classe au grand
...une des écoles de Francfort · Architekt
...chuette. Foto Dr. Wolff

DIE NEUE DORFSCHULE

26
Grundriß im Erdgelchoß · Plan of ground
floor · Plan du rez-de-chaussée · Aus der
Broschüre: Die Neue Dorfschule von Dr.
Franz Kade und Eugen Kaufmann. Verlag
Moritz Diesterweg, Frankfurt a. M. 1930
From the brochure "The new Village School",
by Dr. Franz Kade and Eugen Kaufmann,
published by Messrs. Moritz Diesterweg,
Frankfort-on-Main, 1930 · Pris de la brochure
«La nouvelle école rurale», par le Dr. Franz
Kade and Eugen Kaufmann, publiée par la
maison Moritz Diesterweg, Francforts. M. 1930

ENTWURF ZU EINER EINKLASSIGEN DORFSCHULE MIT KINDERGARTEN

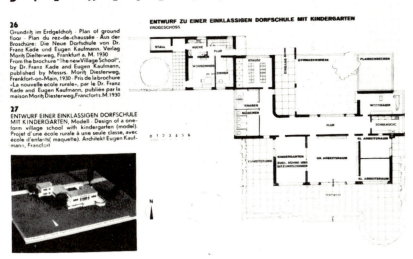

27
ENTWURF EINER EINKLASSIGEN DORFSCHULE
MIT KINDERGARTEN, Modell · Design of a one-
form village school with kindergarten (model).
Projet d'une école rurale à une seule classe, avec
école d'enfants(maquette). Architekt Eugen Kaufmann, Francfort

...der ganzen Anlage. Die drei Pavillons
...tte 1930 ausgeführt. Der Flügel rechts
...gebaut · Plan of the whole institution.
...pavilions in the centre were erected in
...ne on the right wing will be so in 1931
...de l'institution. Les trois pavillons au
...nt construits en 1931, celui à l'aile
...ra en 1931

...SCHULE FRANKFURT - PRAUNHEIM.
...der Rückleite · Backview · Vue d'arrière
...chonn

It is generally accepted that Nikolaus Pevsner is the critic and historian who has interpreted and drawn together their arguments most lucidly. His book, *Pioneers of Modern Design,** is of cardinal importance for anyone who wants to understand the origins of the modern movement. In it he sets out clearly the nature of the ideological building blocks that eventually went into the foundation of that most important of all design schools – the Bauhaus. It flourished in

* *'Pioneers of Modern Design', Nikolaus Pevsner, Penguin Books, 1936 (revised edition 1960).*

Germany during the liberal chaos of the Weimar Republic. When Hitler destroyed German democracy he closed the school and so spread its influence all over the world.

Here are two short extracts from Pevsner's book. Taken together they catch perfectly the polemical nature of the modern movement. They also display the confidence that its practitioners had in their ability to create the environment that people needed in order to live an ordered, agreeable and progressive existence in a technological world:

In Germany the most important architect during those years (1900–1914) was Peter Behrens (1868–1940). Characteristically of the situation about 1900, he began as a painter and underwent the 'moral' reformation towards the applied arts, before he trained as an architect. The applied arts, when Behrens started, meant Art Nouveau. He soon escaped from its enervating atmosphere. His first building, his own house in Darmstadt (1901), already shows a hardening of the tender curves of Art Nouveau. In the same year, Behrens designed a type face in which the change is complete. The curves are straightened, and ornamental initials are decorated with squares and circles only.

His principal buildings before the war he designed for the AEG, one of the big German electrical combines, of which the managing director, P Jordan, had appointed him architect and adviser. In 1909 the turbine factory was built, perhaps the most beautiful industrial building ever erected up to that time. The steel frame is clearly exhibited; wide, perfectly spaced glass panes replace the walls on the side and in the middle of the ends; and if the corners are still expressed by heavy stone with banded rustication and rounded at the angles, the metal frame projecting its sharp corners above these stone pylons redresses the balance boldly and effectively. This design has nothing in common with the ordinary factories of that time, not even the most functional American ones of Albert Kahn with their exposed steel frames. Here for the first time the imaginative possibilities of industrial architecture were visualised. The result is a pure work of architecture, so finely balanced that the huge dimensions are scarcely realised, unless one looks at the people in the street for comparison. The two-storeyed aisle on the left has the flat roof and the row of windows which we find in all the most advanced works of that time.

Notice how Pevsner identifies certain aesthetic and structural characteristics as being progressive. Behrens is said to have 'escaped' from the 'enervating' atmosphere of Art Nouveau. The change is completed when he uses only squares and circles. In the great turbine building 'the steel frame is clearly exhibited' and he introduced the 'flat roof and row of windows which we find in all the most *advanced* works of that time'. This way of speaking catches authentically the moral tone that pervaded the whole movement. Pevsner again displays it eloquently when, at the end of *Pioneers of*

Above and right
Two views of the small model factory designed by Gropius in 1914 for the exhibition of the Deutsche Werkbund. It is a building that displays many features which became characteristics of the modern movement in design.
(The Building Centre)

Modern Design, he discusses a climactic 'modern' building designed by Gropius:

For the Werkbund Exhibition of 1914, Gropius built a small model factory. The north side is his comment on his master's turbine factory of five years before. The reduction of motifs to an absolute minimum and the sweeping simplification of outline are patent. The replacement of Behrens's heavy corner piers by thin metallic lines is specially impressive. Bolder still is the south front with the superb contrast between the decidedly Wrightian brick centre and the completely glazed corners. In the middle there are only the narrowest slits for the windows and the lowest entrance; at the corner, where according to all standards of the past, a sufficient-looking supporting force should show itself, there is nothing but glass encasing transparently two spiral staircases.

The motif has since been imitated as often as the girderless corner of the Fagus Factory; and it shows that Gropius's personal expression by no means lacks grace. There is something sublime in this effortless mastery of material and weight. Never since the Sainte-Chapelle and the choir of Beauvais had the human art of building been so triumphant over matter. Yet the character of the new building is entirely un-Gothic, anti-Gothic. While in the thirteenth century all lines, functional though they were, served the one artistic purpose of pointing heavenwards to a goal beyond this world, and walls were made translucent to carry the transcendental magic of saintly figures rendered in coloured glass, the glass walls are now clear and without mystery, the steel frame is hard, and its expression discourages all other-worldly speculation. It is the creative energy of this world in which we live and work and which we want to master, a world of science and technology, of speed and danger, of hard struggles and no personal security, that is glorified in

Gropius's architecture, and as long as this is the world and these are its ambitions and problems, the style of Gropius and the other pioneers will be valid . . .

The claim is a large one. Elsewhere in his book, Pevsner berates not only the public craving after 'the surprising and fantastic, and for an escape out of reality into a fairy world' but also the architect for craving after 'individual expression'. The cool logic of what we have erroneously come to call 'functionalism' is presented as the only medicine capable of doing us good; as the only architecture truly 'real' in a modern world.

Inevitably these ideas have now come under attack. It is easy enough to accept that the concept of functionalism lives on as a basic part of the history and philosophy of design. Clearly, the impetus of functional theory was decisive in many ways. For example, it can be said to have led to the emergence of a design profession possessing a coherent philosophy of its own. But the suspicion has grown in recent years that, for all their apparent rationalism, the pioneers simply produced another aesthetic style. And the most damning criticism of all those now offered is that their visual masterpieces have not had a beneficial influence on the everyday environment of ordinary people.

Today there are even critics who are ready to question the reality of the revolutionary, reforming role of Gropius and his contemporaries. This is largely the result of efforts to reach a better understanding of the nineteenth century. As we focus more on engineering and humble mass-produced objects, so the eclectic 'high' styles of the Victorian period seem less important. There is also the point that, particularly in Britain and Scandinavia, many designers have continued to be inspired as much by the values of traditional building and handcraftsmanship as by anything that came out of the Bauhaus.

These themes are drawn together lucidly in a book by Herwin Schaefer called *The Roots of Modern Design*.* It is quite explicitly a challenge to the accepted history of the modern movement, and particularly to the interpretation in Pevsner's key work. In essence, what Schaefer has to say is this: the real ancestry of modern design can be found in the simple, practical vernacular of the past, not in the particular historical style that was

* *'The Roots of Modern Design', Herwin Schaefer, Studio Vista, 1970.*

functionalism. Of the functional *style* he writes:

We are able to see now that what we called modern functional design and considered a new and lasting order, because it seemed based on reason, was but a moment in which function was the proclaimed rationale for a style based, in practice, on a predilection for geometric forms – the Platonic forms of cone, circle, square – avidly avowed as a dogma by its creators, and made into a formula by its practitioners.

But for the vernacular, and its practical functionalism, a far more important role is set out. It is identified as the genuine grass roots of modern design, and its development in the nineteenth century is seen, in a sense, as *the* history of design. Its relationship with functional style is described in this way:

One must . . . point out the irony in a period (the 1920s and 30s) that proclaimed function as the determinant of form and yet was guided by formal values outside the consideration of function. Actually, the functional tradition existed side by side with the functional style, as well as having been absorbed into it. The functional *tradition* existed as a matter of course in areas remote from style and fashion, its products being timelessly modern; the functional *style* was a conscious and deliberate effort, a matter of aesthetic concern, accepted by informed and fashionable taste, but modern in the stylistic sense and not necessarily in the sense of being timeless.

To my mind Schaefer's semantic argument is proven. The distinction between the tradition and the style is a useful one. But this does not mean that we must dismiss the creative contribution made by the pioneers of modern design. The moral dimension

of their work will be important in the future evolution of the design professions and, in terms of structure and aesthetics, their buildings and products are often unassailable. What is more, Schaefer accepts something that I would myself find tendentious: I do not believe that functionalism, in the utilitarian sense, is particularly characteristic of modernity.

What we might rather say is that, since the Industrial Revolution, design, like the whole of culture, has been, at one and the same time, utilitarian and expressionistic. Or, to put it another way, that the functionalist tradition has always co-existed with an alternative that is romantic and escapist. The physical structure of the modern world is essentially a blend of each of these contradictory forces.

TRICKIER EVEN THAN "THE INVISIBLE MAN" AND MORE SENSATIONAL IN ITS NOVEL TWIST

CARL LAEMMLE presents

LOWELL SHERMAN'S UPROARIOUS PRODUCTION

of THORNE SMITH'S AMAZING NOVEL

NIGHT LIFE of the GODS

with
ALAN MOWBRAY
PEGGY SHANNON
RICHARD CARLE
FLORINE McKINNEY
WESLEY BARRY
HENRY ARMETTA
WILLIAM (stage) BOYD
ROBERT WARWICK

ABOVE IS A REPRODUCTION OF THE 48 SHEET STAND

But what *is* design? What is the positive element that results in a building, toothbrush, railway engine, or dishwasher? The stock answer, that it is a creative act, is true but is itself something of a mystery. Few people are clear exactly what being creative is, and individuals like artists and writers, whose whole stock-in-trade is supposedly creativity, find it a baffling concept to explain. Biologically the activity in the brain that supports creative thinking is not clear, and psychologists and educationalists are divided over the best way of fostering creative capacity in children and adults.

Although it is not at the moment easy to clarify the concept of creativity any further, it is possible to say a good deal more about the *kind* of creativity that engages the designer. We can define further the input and the output of the designer's work; we can say in what terms the designer is creative; and we can describe the 'language' or medium in which his creativity finds expression.

As a start it is useful to see just where creativity is needed. First, in general 'problem solving' or the intuitive approach to the project as a whole, whatever it may be. Second, in the actual detailed work of design, which may involve pencil and paper, model making or just thinking. The first is, if you like, the strategy of design; the second the tactics. It would be easy and neat to be able to say that two entirely different kinds of creativity are involved. There does not, at first sight, appear to be a great deal in common between the 'problem solving' aspect of the strategy and the more practical and aesthetic nature of the tactics. But the division is completely unreal and it is clear that in the designer's mind the two parts are indissolubly linked. It is a characteristic of design thinking that any 'solution' to a problem is embodied in the guise of a distinctive material object – the object *is* the solution, and comes complete with the designer's handwriting indelibly upon it.

It is this that distinguishes design from invention. Invention is concerned with abstract principles that are, on the whole, separable from the device that happens to embody them. The character of design, on the other hand, is to be found solely in its material embodiment. Take as an example the wheel: the principle of the invention can be found in all wheels, but design is separately and distinctively involved in every different form of wheel that has been made. There is no real element of design in the abstract principle of the wheel, only in this wheel or that wheel.

It follows that design activity is very much bound up with what is called style, or at least that style is a large part of the medium in which the designer's own particular brand of creativity operates. A design is always particular and finite, bound by a culture and by the visual repertoire of a period. But style is not meretricious – it isn't 'styling' – it is a fundamental aspect of thought and civilisation, deeply affecting the character and feeling of life at any particular time. Style provides the framework for the designer's mode of thought, and it is at once a limitation and a stimulus. It effectively joins the work done in the past with the work that will be done in the future and, although the designer may be inevitably trapped by a style, he can also add to it and transform it. Style does not stay still, it develops as men respond to changes in society and technology, and its operation can easily be identified in any group of man-made objects, even if they are as apparently rational as a railway engine or an aeroplane.

But it is possible to be even more precise. Within the idea of style, the designer's creativity is based on visual qualities like form, colour and texture that, taken together, make up a language providing the basis for a self-contained and important way of thinking. It is only because of the general unfamiliarity with non-literary forms that the designer often has to 'translate' from this medium of communication to another. The fact that his thinking is not based on words does not invalidate it. Just as a composer works directly and fully with sounds, so the designer can operate completely in his own terms of 'design' thought.

Design is not invention. There is no real
element of design in abstract principles,
only in principles that are embodied in
buildings or products or proposals for
them. All the electric fires shown here are
based on the one basic invention for
supplying heat, but each is a different
design with its own characteristic
handwriting.

Right
One of the earliest Belling electric fires,
1912.

Far right
First Belling imitation coal electric
fire, *1921.*

Below
A Ferranti design using wrought iron
fire dogs to support an electric fire.
1920s.

Below right
A Belling fire dating from the *1930s.*
(Design Council)

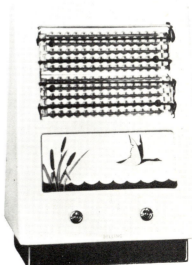

As a part of the Design in General Education project at the Royal College of Art, Professor Bruce Archer attempted to give a more precise description of the core of design activity by relating it to two other great streams of human endeavour: language and science:*

When we look at humanities, we find that many people will argue that the core subject is language, and the body of knowledge is literature. In science the core subject might be said to be mathematics while the body of knowledge is the laws within which the mathematical mode is applied. In those terms, I would argue that the body of knowledge in design is the man-made habitat: architecture, the contents of the Victoria and Albert Museum, what is in the galleries and fashion shows. It is there, not in books, but all around. I would go on to say that our core subject is modelling . . . Here I am using the term in a very strict sense of the word. A model is something which stands for or represents something else. This is the core concept in design. In the simplest sense it is exactly what a plan or a design is. A model of this kind may be created for a variety of purposes. It may be used in order to simplify, in order to understand, in order to manipulate, in order to test. It can be descriptive or it can be prescriptive. It can say what things ought to be like, such as an architect's drawing, or it can be predictive, like a model of the economy telling us when we are all going to go bust . . .
    In the areas in which we are interested, modelling and the ways in which we deal with it are manifold. Drawing is a kind of model. The drawing stands for or represents something else. That applies as much to representational drawing as it does to technical drawing . . . Computing has arisen out of the use of electric current

as an analogue of something else. A knitting pattern is a model of a special kind: an algorithm. Flow charts, diagrams, graphs: these are all kinds of models.

This idea of 'modelling' is of special importance in design because the designer is always concerned with the future. He is, in fact, attempting to decide what a particular aspect of the future will be like. He is giving form to it, and colour and texture. Thus, he is dealing with change. Unless a change were envisaged and desired, there would be nothing needing to be modelled; no decisions about the future would be needed because things would go on as before. Modelling, in this sense, is the tool that makes it possible to make hypotheses about the future, to test them, to communicate them to others, and – eventually – to realise them in the guise of buildings and products. The designer's repertoire of models is extremely large. A number, taken from the work involved in designing a new hospital, are illustrated on the next few pages.

In any project a designer will use many ways of 'modelling' in order to understand what he is doing; to represent the activities he is designing for; and to create and foresee the future character of buildings or products. Shown here, and on pages 58 to 63, are examples of 'models' that were used during the design of the new Greenwich District Hospital. They are taken from two books 'Hospital Research and Briefing Problems' and 'Hospital Traffic and Supply Problems' published by King Edward's Hospital Fund for London.

Right
A diagram made to clarify the way in which the design work for the project would be organised and how proposals and decisions would travel from group to group of those involved.

Far right above
A thumbnail sketch exploring, in the broadest possible terms, the alternative types of corridor system (X, H and T) that could be adopted in the proposed hospital.

Far right below
A rough sketch used to clarify the likely traffic flows between the various parts of the hospital catering facilities.

* 'Summer School Papers', Royal College of Art, 1976.

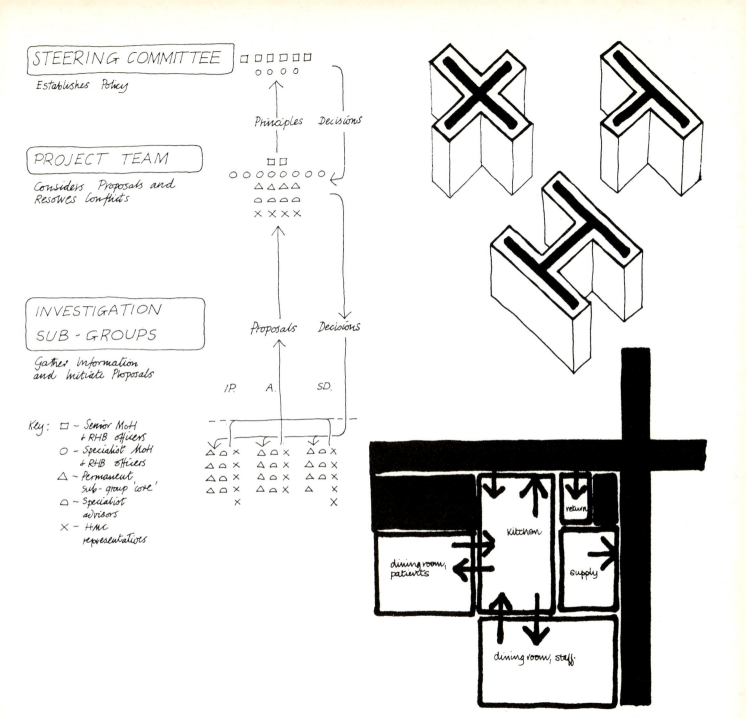

STEERING COMMITTEE

Establishes Policy

Principles   Decisions

PROJECT TEAM

Considers Proposals and
Resolves Conflicts

Proposals   Decisions

INVESTIGATION
SUB - GROUPS

Gather Information
and Initiate Proposals

I.P.   A.   S.D.

Key: □ ~ Senior MoH
       & RHB officers
     O ~ Specialist MoH
       & RHB officers
     △ ~ Permanent
       sub-group 'core'
     ◠ ~ Specialist
       advisors
     X ~ HMC
       representatives

Kitchen

return

dining room,
patients

supply

dining room, staff.

SIMPLIFIED ANALYSIS OF HANDLING OPTIONS IN AND AROUND THE MAIN STORE

ASSUMPTIONS: ONLOADING AND STACKING TIME — 200 UNITS PER MAN/HOUR
CARRYING OR PUSHING TIME 200 FEET PER MINUTE

① HAND OPERATION. — 3.8 MAN/HOURS.

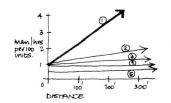

② TWO-WHEELED HAND TRUCK — 1.6 MAN/HOURS.

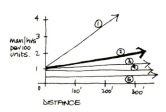

③ FOUR WHEELED HAND TRUCK. — 1.8 MAN/HOURS.

④ CONVEYOR BELT. — 1.0 MAN/HOURS (EQUIVALENT)

⑤ MANUAL OPERATED PALLET TRUCK — 0.3 MAN/HOURS.
OR FORK LIFT TRUCK.

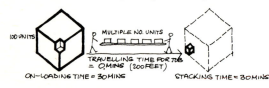

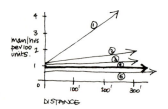

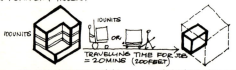

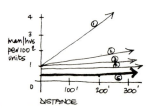

Left
Sketch diagrams and graphs made to help clarify and explain the characteristics of alternative methods of handling deliveries to the hospital's main store.

Opposite page
Top left
Drawing made to help clarify the necessary relationship between door and corridor widths where beds will have to be moved from area to area.

Below left
How high can we store things? Shelf heights in relation to the reach of a man and a woman of average height.

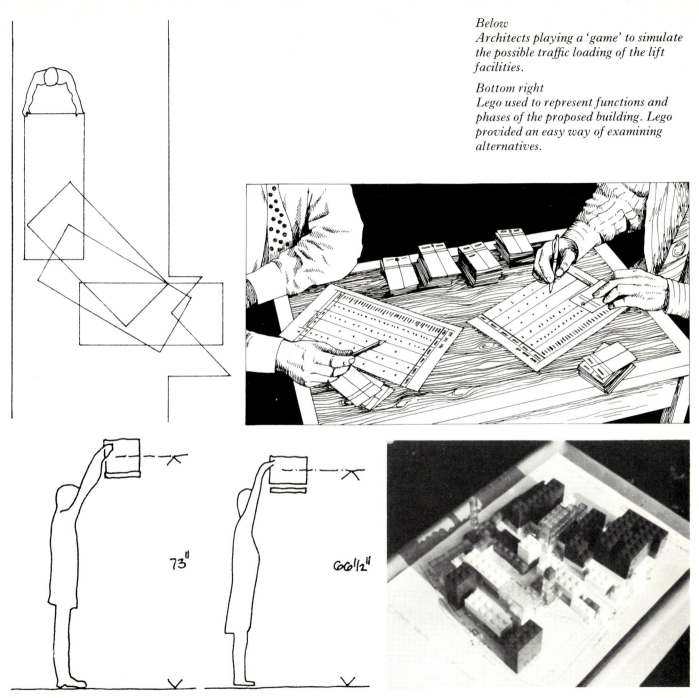

Below
Architects playing a 'game' to simulate the possible traffic loading of the lift facilities.

Bottom right
Lego used to represent functions and phases of the proposed building. Lego provided an easy way of examining alternatives.

73"

66½"

Right
Adaptable model used for investigating alternative designs for the layout of rooms.

Below
A detailed model that was made to represent the proposed positioning of the engineering services and plant.

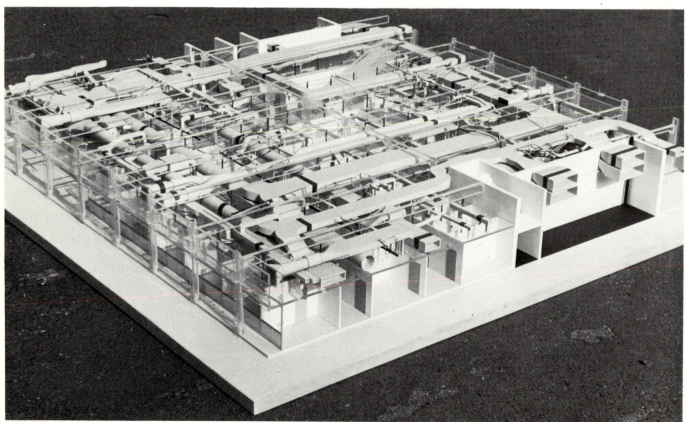

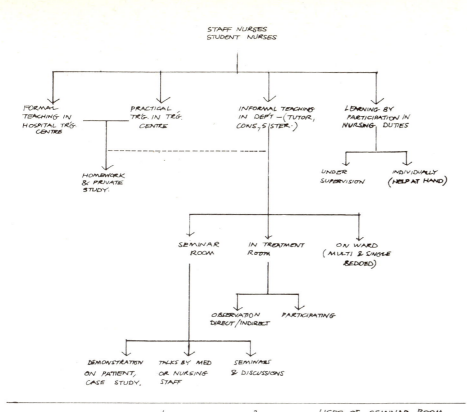

STAFF NURSES
STUDENT NURSES

FORMAL TEACHING IN HOSPITAL TRG. CENTRE

PRACTICAL TRG. IN TRG. CENTRE

INFORMAL TEACHING IN DEPT — (TUTOR, CONS, SISTER.)

LEARNING BY PARTICIPATION IN NURSING DUTIES

HOMEWORK & PRIVATE STUDY.

UNDER SUPERVISION

INDIVIDUALLY (HELP AT HAND)

SEMINAR ROOM

IN TREATMENT ROOM

ON WARD (MULTI & SINGLE BEDDED)

OBSERVATION DIRECT/INDIRECT

PARTICIPATING

DEMONSTRATION ON PATIENT, CASE STUDY.

TALKS BY MED OR NURSING STAFF

SEMINARS & DISCUSSIONS

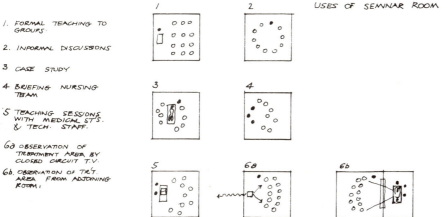

USES OF SEMINAR ROOM

1. FORMAL TEACHING TO GROUPS.

2. INFORMAL DISCUSSIONS

3 CASE STUDY

4 BRIEFING NURSING TEAM

5 TEACHING SESSIONS WITH MEDICAL ST'S. & TECH. STAFF.

6a OBSERVATION OF TREATMENT AREA BY CLOSED CIRCUIT T.V.

6b. OBSERVATION OF TR'T. AREA FROM ADJOINING ROOM.

IN PATIENT CARE. G.D.H.	M.O.H. Architects Branch	IP/29
TRAINING, NURSES. USES OF SEMINAR RM. Ref. 3/7 5/2		

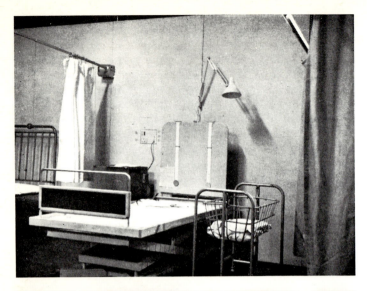

Top left
A full size mock-up of the proposed bed
area layout. It was used for testing
whether or not it would meet the
requirements of nurses and patients.

Below left
A prototype of the structural system
being erected for testing and
evaluation.

Above and opposite page
Photographs of the finished hospital
taken by Chris Ridley.

There is a further question we can ask ourselves about these models. We have seen that they are directed at the future. We have seen that they are about deciding the form, colour and texture of the world we inhabit. And we have seen that this world is itself an expression of the diversity of human aspirations, material and spiritual. The matrix is growing. But what, in more specific terms, is the content that the designer manipulates in his models and that finds expression in what is eventually produced? What, in today's world, are likely to be the immediate ingredients of a typical piece of design activity?

Although each particular piece of work a designer does is quite distinct in the problems it presents, it is possible to point out three key elements that are involved in every case and that, in the end, determine the area of choice open to the designer. These three elements are function, finance and available materials, but it is important to remember that they combine to present a total design situation that can only be properly resolved as a whole. So much is talked about function, and associated words like efficiency and performance, that it might be thought that this was the most clear-cut aspect of the designer's job – to make things work well. It is true that primary aims like shelter, comfort and mobility are easily enough described, but the terms in which they can be realised are affected by changes in society and technology. Function only makes sense in relation to particular needs and particular resources for meeting them; it is not an absolute quality related to one particular way of doing

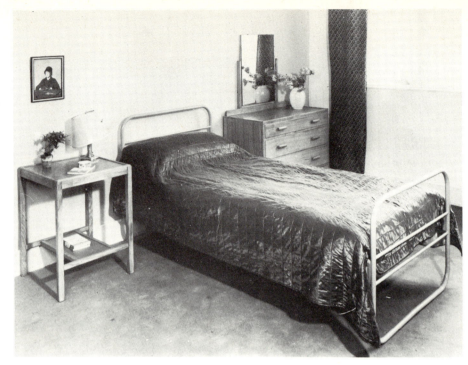

things. An object is only 'functional' in the context of a defined human need, a defined level of technology, and a defined cultural background.

As we have seen, the adjective 'functional' has become linked with a style of design rather than with the fantastically varied requirements of society. This is confusing. The functionalist claim that 'form should follow function' is a perfectly valid one, provided that the breadth of possible functions is realised. Where the dictum that form should follow function is cramping and obvious nonsense is when it is related specifically to the idea of using the smallest amount of materials to achieve a given result. The notion of economy in materials is not bad in itself – as a basis for design it has

produced some spectacularly beautiful results – but it is not the only possible approach. In his book *The Nature of Design*,* David Pye argued that even mechanical and structural consideration may sometimes place only very small restrictions on the form of any particular piece of design:

. . . the components must be strong enough to transmit the (necessary) forces or resist them. This requirement obviously affects the size of each component . . . But in these days we are apt to forget what a very slight restriction on shape the calculation of structures does actually impose. This is because we take it for granted first of all that the minimum amount of material

* *'The Nature of Design', David Pye, Studio Vista, 1964.*

PHYSIOGNOMICK CAUDLE PORTRAITS.

London Published by William Spooner, 377, Strand

What is functional? It depends on your aspirations and your resources!

Opposite
A simple bed with tubular head and foot.
(Design Council)

Above left
A fantasy bed in the Chinese manner said to be by Thomas Chippendale.
(Crown Copyright. Victoria and Albert Museum)

Above right
Thwarted aspirations. A satirical print from the nineteenth century.
(John Johnson Collection, Bodleian Library)

ought to be used (a cheese-paring attitude which fortunately did not hold in, for instance, Rome, Athens, Venice, Chartres, and a few other places), and because we habitually use standard prefabricated components when making structures. The fact that you have calculated the minimum cross-section necessary to a member such as a column need not often prevent you from making it any shape you like.

This is important because it is the designer's responsibility to look more deeply at the needs of society than is suggested by the idea simply of solving material problems by rational engineering. The environment is the home of mén's hopes, aspirations and fears, just as much as it is the home of their physical bodies. The function of an object is a complex thing, and it is important that the designer should be able also to consider the wider implications of innovation in terms of technology or design.

It should be clear by now that function, as it applies to designers today, is a very difficult concept to describe and that, taken in its broadest sense, it could involve our whole view of what society should be like. What we shall see next is that the degree to which any particular function is achieved is controlled, to an extraordinarily large extent, by the other two factors – finance and available materials. Although a desired function is obviously the most important thing that a designer has to consider, his solution can only be realistic in terms of what technology will allow, how much it will cost and how much it is worth.

One of the weaknesses of design criticism and philosophy in the past has been the way in which they have

persistently ignored the effects of economics on design. The extreme simplicity and 'truth to materials' which the modern movement advocated were not only a 'machine aesthetic' and a 'reaction against debased decoration', but an attempt to create a way of achieving quality within the economic limitations of mass production. Economics determine the designer's freedom of action at every point and, to a greater or lesser degree, have partly determined the character of men's artefacts all through history. Professor Pye goes so far as to identify economics as the *major* factor in design:

It (the idea of function) has diverted attention from the fact that those influences (which limit the shape of designed things independently of the designer's preference) are many, disparate, and of various effects, and particularly from the fact that economy, not physics, is always the predominant influence because directly and indirectly it sets the most limits.

Of course, economy in this sense is not by any means the same thing as the precise financial problems facing a particular company in asking a designer to develop a particular product. But money in these very direct terms is an expression of the more complicated group of considerations that Professor Pye calls economy:

Theoretically it is possible to design for a result without the design being influenced in any degree, either directly or indirectly, by economy. In practice this does not happen . . . But . . . economy implies something more than saving money.

Any change originated by man exacts a

cost from him. The cost is reckoned in effort, trouble, time, often in running risk and enduring discomfort also. Adam found this out.

Economy . . . must be understood as referring primarily to this unpleasant catalogue and only secondarily to the money which we pay to avoid enduring it; for when we pay a price in money for a device, as a rule we are paying directly or indirectly to escape the natural cost in effort or discomfort, trouble, time or risk, of the result which the device gives.

The great majority of devices simply enable us to get cut-price results. There are really rather few devices which make it possible to get results which without them would be impossible . . .

This brings out two important points. First, that it is inherent in the very idea of design that a 'costable' benefit of some kind will result. Second, that the realistic estimate of a piece of design is 'what is it worth?' rather than 'what does it cost?', and that 'being too expensive' only makes sense in relation to an assessment of value. 'Is it worth the money?' is the real question.

It is easy to see that economic considerations must be related to the third factor of available materials. If we interpret this in the broadest sense as meaning available technology, as well as actual construction media like plastics or wood, we are talking about one of the fundamental elements that determine cost. In fact, the cost of a particular material or technique is what decides whether or not it is available to the designer in any given situation. This is more subtle than it seems, for decisions can seldom be taken in relation to completely rational arguments about function and hypothetical economics. Unless a new factory or plant is being set up, the

What is functional? A cake is for eating? This is a cake for celebrating. Royal wedding cake from the collection of photographs in the Royal Library at Windsor.
(Reproduced by gracious permission of Her Majesty the Queen)

What is functional? Clothes are to keep warm in? To keep the wet out? These clothes are for a great ceremony: they are symbolic. Royal wedding group from the collection of photographs in the Royal Library at Windsor.
(Reproduced by gracious permission of Her Majesty the Queen)

designer is almost certain to be faced with a reservoir of existing men and machinery that will be biased towards certain ways of doing things. It is generally more economic to build on this basis, and it may be an important part of the designer's job to recognise the highest standards that can be reached with the existing resources and then work towards them.

There is a strong negative link between innovation, as expressed in the availability of special technology, and demand. Only where there is a huge market does it become feasible for the designer to think in terms of setting up completely new installations perfectly adapted to the job in hand. But the wider the market, the more difficult it will be to sell an entirely revolutionary product. Manufacturers are naturally nervous about making vast commitments of capital and expertise on experimental projects; they prefer to launch a new idea on a small scale to test reaction first. At once this means that the capital available is limited. The situation is a merry-go-round that is only broken in, say, the armaments industry where failure to make a big technological and financial commitment to innovation would be completely disastrous.

Cedric Price, the architect, says that the building industry has been extraordinarily unable to demand technological advance on its own account. The architect depends on techniques and discoveries that originate from technological work in other fields like engineering and space research; the architect himself cannot call for any very expensive research directed to his own specific problems. Much the same is true of the product

What is functional? Tables and chairs designed to meet very different social and economic situations.

Above
The 'Turkish style' in a 'gentleman's corner' illustrated in Queen magazine at the turn of the century.

Opposite
Boxes in Covent Garden photographed by Chris Ridley.

designer, though not in every field. Again it is a question of cost and investment linked to demand and potential profits.

We said at the beginning of this discussion that the three determining elements to be found in every design problem – function, finance, and available materials – would, in any real situation, be related together, and that they had to be resolved as a unity. This is true, but it is salutary to be aware of the impossibility of achieving anything that might be called a 'perfect' outcome. In the nature of things the resolution of conflicting requirements produces a makeshift; all men's constructive efforts are to a degree ridiculous, to a degree splendid, and inevitably temporary. Professor Pye says:

The requirements for design conflict and cannot be reconciled. All designs for devices are in some degree failures, either because they flout one or other of the requirements or because they are compromises, and compromise implies a degree of failure . . .

The designer or his client has to choose in what degree and where there shall be failure. Thus the shape of all designed things is the product of arbitrary choice. If you vary the terms of your compromise – say, more speed, more heat, less safety, more discomfort, lower first cost – then you vary the shape of the thing designed. It is quite impossible for any design to be the 'logical outcome of the requirements' simply because, the requirements being in conflict, their logical outcome is an impossibility . . .

Among a number of examples he takes the case of the more or less standard dimensions of a small, cheaply produced table:

The requirements for a low first cost may conflict with the requirements of use and access, as may be seen in the case of a small table, which needs to be fairly cheap, fairly light and yet steady on its legs. The use of wood makes these things possible. Experience has shown that the method of constructing tables which gives the most steadiness for the least money and weight is what one finds in a kitchen table – four legs, four rails, and a top. The illustration shows the corner of it. It is no more an ideal solution than any other design, but it works pretty well . . .

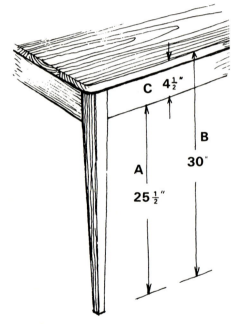

The dimensions of the more or less standard small, cheaply produced kitchen table. They represent a compromise between the various desirable qualities for an object of this kind – a balance between function, cost and available materials.
(From 'The Nature of Design' by David Pye published by Studio Vista Ltd)

Several million people have used such tables to eat at and write at in the last two hundred years and very few if any are known to have been much the worse for it. The dimensions shown are a compromise. It would be nicer if A were two or three inches bigger, so that you could cross your legs; and if B were two or three inches smaller so that the table top was nearer your lap. But C cannot be much less if the table is to be cheap and steady and durable, so you must put up with A being rather small and B being rather large.'

The chances are that a completely fresh approach – new materials giving similar strength for less bulk, a lower standard of production or what have you – might produce a different result, but it is certain that the new set-up would contain its own inherent compromises. In other words, design is partly a balancing act; a decision on conflicting aims each of which may be desirable in itself. This does not mean that what we might call 'real design' is a myth, for this activity of compromise is inherent in design, and it is clearly the designer's responsibility to arrive at the best conceivable balance of priorities.

The aim of this chapter has been to review some of the answers that might be given to the question 'What is design?' This has been done in such a way as to focus on those aspects that may have special significance for teachers of various kinds. Thus, the discussion has travelled from some of the philosophical issues to a more detailed review of the content and nature of design activity. On the way, design has been identified as an historical phenomenon embracing an astonishingly wide range of human concerns, aspirations and sensibilities. In the next chapter an attempt will be made to look more closely at some of the social and political problems that are related to design and through these to understand something of the connexion between design and the community. In Chapter 4, these two themes will be brought together in a more detailed discussion of the significance of design as an educational medium.

But this chapter also needs rounding off. It needs to be pointed more precisely towards teachers and children. What we can say in this respect is something like this: for the teacher, design can best be conceived of as being about creating the future. Thought of in this way it can be seen as being to do with deciding how we want to live in relation to the skills and resources at our disposal. But because our resources are limited and our skills are finite, it is also about compromise, it is about making the most of what we have in every aspect of its, and our, potentialities. It is about what kind of physical world we want to inhabit and so, essentially and precisely, it is about ourselves and our understanding of ourselves. It is at this point that design really begins to be of interest to teachers.

Old Oak
(Greater London Council houses)

Chapter 3

Design in the community

Design today has to be understood not as a separate, solely practical activity but as a part of the whole effort to make a workable and effective culture for modern industrial society. In medieval Europe, art and architecture played their part in the broader pattern of the preoccupations of that time. In the twentieth century, design has its part to play in the broad pattern of a developing material equality. In the middle ages, art pictured the hierarchical world from God to serf, now design is the key to the humanisation of our environment – feeding the mental and physical growth of a mass society. This has been recognised in many ways. Since 1900 a new awareness of the problems involved has slowly spread, creating new schools of design and architecture. Between the two World Wars the Bauhaus in Germany provided a focus for experiment and creation that has had an influence practically all over Europe and America. A new approach to design has come into being that aspires to use industry as the tool aiming at better conditions of life. Yet there are deep and valid objections to the nature of the man-made world that has been created as a result of these ideals. It is important for teachers to examine this problem and to attempt to give young people the means for understanding it. And, if necessary, the means for changing it.

There is a quite startling ignorance among ordinary people of the nature of the world that has grown out of the Industrial Revolution and, perhaps as a result, a quite startling dislike for it as well. The community, indeed, has been an ostrich; it has liked to think that new ways of meeting old needs would leave the needs and the world unchanged, but this has not happened, and human institutions have not kept pace with the resulting upheavals.

The motorcar is the classic example of this. What was originally thought of as simply an extension of the old need to move from place to place has grown into something that has changed the whole balance between town and country and posed huge problems for urban planners. But cars are just the most obvious of thousands of devices that, taken together, add up to a completely new situation. Television has changed the whole balance of entertainment; telecommunications have made knowledge and information available throughout the world on a scale that has had a direct impact on the nature of diplomacy and politics. With the coming of computers, even thought and its development are becoming completely bound up with devices external to man himself. It appears to be certain that the impact of technology on life is not simply to make possible more of the same; the vast scale of what is happening means that we are witnessing a social and environmental change comparable to

Left
Corner shop in East London,
photographed in 1965.
(Chris Ridley)

'Yet there are deep and valid objections
to the man-made world that has been
created as a result of these ideals.'

Left
Corner shop in East London,
photographed in 1965.
(Chris Ridley)

Right
Modern housing designed as a
replacement for decaying Victorian
slums. This surburban environment has
many advantages over its nineteenth
century urban predecessor, but the high
degree of standardisation that results
from industrialisation and the lack of
individuality can cause unhappiness in
people who grew up in a less hygienic but
more intimate atmosphere.

that which marks off the middle ages from the Renaissance.

What is it all about? As has already been suggested, it is about the extension of man's power. This is easy to say but hard to understand; where exactly is power being extended and what effect is it having?

In September 1971, John McHale published a review of *World Facts and Trends*.* This was a statistical

* 'World Facts and Trends', John McHale, 'Futures', Vol 3, No 3, September 1971.

summary of major environmental developments on planet earth, many traced back to medieval times and beyond. He looked at things like the increase in speed of travel; technological innovation; life expectancy; speed of communication; the increase in explosive and killing power; and the increasing disturbance of natural systems by man. Of the changes that had gathered momentum since the Industrial Revolution he said:

The last third of the twentieth century has become increasingly characterised as the age of critical transition, of revolution and discontinuity . . . Our present waves of change differ not only in their quantitative aspects from those of the recent past, *but also in the quality and degree of their inter-relationships.* [My italics]

McHale pointed to two major aspects of change which he found crucial:

One is the explosive growth in man's actual and potential capacities to interfere

on a large scale with the natural environmental processes.

His second aspect struck directly at cultural problems:

The other is the lag in conceptual orientation towards these capacities and in the cognitive understanding of the social processes through which we may manage change more effectively. In both cases the conceptual grasp of the rate and magnitude of ongoing changes and their potential consequences has emerged as one of our prior survival imperatives.

He then picked out the following characteristics as being of special significance:

Increased frequency The new relationships and narrowing intervals between scientific discovery, technological development, and large-scale usage has become dramatically visible only in the past few decades.

Range and scale In addition to this reverberative increase in the frequency of change factors, many of the long-range and large-scale effects of various types of change on the environment, on social relations, on health, etc, have only become measurably apparent in the same period.

Size and complexity The question of the size, distribution, and complexity of many of our technological systems components is an important factor here. With increased size come vastly increased dangers of hazard to larger numbers of people and larger areas of the environment. We have recently viewed an increasing number of near catastrophes in terms of oil spills, radiation leakages, large aircraft

Above
Modern Birmingham. Here is a vivid contrast in environments. The streets of the railway age are in the foreground; the new shopping and commercial centre, products of the age of the motor-car, are in the background. Society has not been particularly good at planning ahead for the effects of such technological changes.
(Chris Ridley)

Opposite
'The extension of man's power.' The huge scale of operations of modern technology is symbolised by this network of conveyors and walkways. The power of technology to affect the environment places heavy responsibilities on designers of every kind.
(Chris Ridley)

Above
The 'magic carpet' of speedy communications. This early advertisement for Thomas Cook stands for the variety of ways in which technological change travels quickly from one part of the world to another. As a result, such changes affect life everywhere, often in unpredictable and unwanted ways. (Thomas Cook)

crashes, thalidomide-type chemical poisoning, large-scale power failures, etc.

Expanded impact and awareness
Through increase in the speed of transportation and communication, the agencies of change (ideas, artifacts [sic], techniques, images, and attitudes) are now diffused more rapidly and penetrate more swiftly into more aspects of human life.

Differential rates Changes in technologies, in ideas, institutional and social changes, occur at varying rates and have different time spans of integration and acceptance, causing dissonance and discontinuity in and between various sectors of society.

Many would argue that, against such a demanding background, the community is ill equipped with institutions capable of handling change effectively and, further, that the design professions themselves deploy a range of attitudes and skills that are inadequate to the task.

It is to the economist Adam Smith, who died in 1790, that we have to look for one of the first convincing codifications of the designer's role in industrial society. Smith summed up the significance of the economic and technological forces that had been gathering strength since medieval times. In his treatment of mass production and the division of labour he foreshadowed with complete accuracy the emergence of the designer as a part of the modern world of highly educated specialists. Here, in a single quote from a draft of of his famous book *The Wealth of Nations*,* is the key:

In opulent and commercial societies . . . to think or to reason comes to be, like every other employment, a particular business, which is carried on by a very few people, who furnish the public with all the thought and reason possessed by the vast multitudes that labour.

In my book *Art in Society*, I attempted to point out some of the social and cultural implications of Smith's vision, which rapidly became the actual condition of society:

Such a high level of generalisation was founded on accurate knowledge of efficient industrial practice. The tendency to specialise which he identified was dramatically effective and destroyed once and for all the old work and craft relations in society. It is unnecessary to be a Marxist to recognise the immense change of human meaning that is involved. In any case, Communist states display exactly the same kind of bureaucratic and alienating structure in their own most 'efficient' enterprises. For us, the salient point is to recognise how rigid and impervious to equality and liberalism is any such vertically organised specialisation. The division of labour does not imply the division of responsibility and power: quite the reverse.

There is, however, the other, triumphant side to the division of labour. *The Wealth of Nations* emphasised what it meant to have hopes of a growth in human prosperity, of a spreading of the enlightenment and a consequent extension of civilisation. Smith predicted with satisfaction that the division of labour was a radical element in society. He saw that a vast increase in productivity, based on technology and modern methods of production, must inevitably change the power relations in society. What he actually predicted was the end of the

* *This extract is quoted from 'Art and the Industrial Revolution', Francis Klingender, Evelyn Adams and Mackay, 1968.*

feudal aristocracy and the rise of the middle classes, not the extension of democracy, but it was, all the same, clearly meant to be the start of an economy of plenty. Smith looked to a time when even the labourer in a civilised community would be better accommodated than 'many an African King, the absolute master of the lives and liberties of ten thousand naked savages'!

Smith argued that when shortage disappeared it would be open to men to extend their other capacities in exactly the same way as the division of labour was already extending their productive capacity.

Any hungry man would agree with Smith about the deforming and destructive aspects of shortage. What is less easy to evaluate is how far the structural inflexibility of industrialisation has been such as to negate the advances that might otherwise be expected from the spread of wealth.

Smith had little to offer on such pressing contemporary problems as pollution and resources, but he did encompass the precise dimensions of the problem of political power facing industrial man. Already, in 1790, he recognised the trade-off that the consumer and citizen still makes today between plenty and involvement, and he identified the interplay between 'bad' work and extended leisure. Smith spelt out the emergence of a social contract based on the existence of boring work and the compensations of vastly extended consumption and entertainment. He penetrated to the core of the modern paradox. The division of labour brought a dramatic increase in economic power for the mass of the people. In this respect it gave more power to the community than before. But with it went the emergence of bureaucratic

specialists, many of them designers of one kind or another, who made decisions on behalf of society and, therefore, controlled its development. In this respect, the community had, and still has, extraordinarily little power to affect very large and important areas of decision making.

Victorian industry created wealth and concentrated power into the hands of a relatively small number of owners, managers and designers in Europe and the United States. Here a Chinese trade delegation, led by His Imperial Highness The Duke Tsai Tse, visits the works of an engineering company in 1906. They are entertained by a group of directors and executives. The photograph is one of many taken in the Midlands by Benjamin Stone. (Reproduced by permission from the Stone Collection of Photographs in Birmingham Reference Library)

*The conundrum of 'bad' work and
'extended' leisure in an industrialised
world.*

Richard, aged 12.
*'Here's how most people spend their
week and it all happens because of
money. Monday morning off you go to
some smelly factory, same every day –
on Friday or payday it isn't so bad –
then on Saturday watch TV or go to a
football match, in the evening go to the
pub or something else like a disco.
Suddenly no more money. Wake up on
Monday morning off you go, to some
smelly old factory . . . If you ask me this
money lark is stupid.'
The quotation is from 'Woman'
magazine for 25 October 1975. It is one
of hundreds collected by writer Anna
Motson who asked young schoolchildren
all over Britain to write down what they
thought about economics and inflation.*

*Right
Work is often repetitive and boring. A
handicapped person assembles
mass-produced components for toys. The
results of her repetitive efforts will
provide the material for play for many
children.
(King Edward's Hospital Fund for
London. Drawn by Don Heywood from
a photograph by Julian Sheppard)*

Work is often inhuman and dangerous, but it produces wealth. This means more for everyone to share, but frequently little of the wealth finds its way into the surroundings of those who do the most difficult work.
(Chris Ridley)

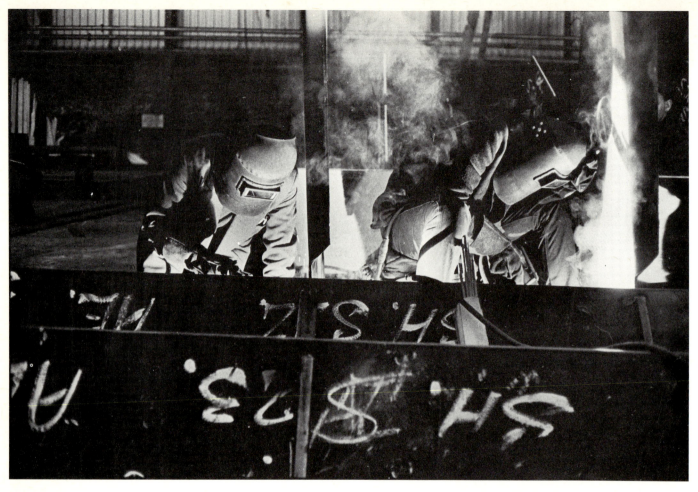

Above and right
The reality of work – experienced as a 'hard' first-hand world of noise and effort (Chris Ridley) – contrasts with the dream of leisure – often experienced as a 'soft' second-hand world of unobtainable fantasy in which, for example, 'Gentlemen Prefer Blondes'. (Still from the film 'Gentlemen Prefer Blondes' by courtesy of Twentieth Century-Fox Film Company Limited)

In a recent broadcast E F Schumacher,* inventor of the famous reformist slogan 'small is beautiful', attempted to spell out just how far our expectations of life and work have been warped and conditioned by the requirements of the division of labour:

Frustration makes people unhappy and often unhealthy. It can make them violent or completely listless. If they cannot feel 'real' while at work, no amount of recreational facilities can help them. As a sensitive British worker put it: 'The factory I work in is part of one of those combines which seem to have an ambition to become the great provider, both in and out of work, for its employees. Recreational facilities abound: but the number of people using them is small in percentage . . . The company bends over backwards to make amends for the lethargy that the factory has produced in the worker. The effect is treated while the cause is ignored.'

Anyone who can say, honestly and convincingly, 'I enjoy my work,' has become an object of astonishment and envy. Work, as the sociologists say, has become purely instrumental. Unlike sport, it is not being undertaken for the joy of it, since, for most people, the joy has gone out of it; it is undertaken as a hateful necessity. This is where modern society has snookered itself. Alienation from work means alienation from reality, for without the reality of work there cannot be the reality of economic well-being. Money incomes are nothing more than a token; the reality behind the token is work: somebody's work. When the work turns sour, the money cannot stay sound.

What answer has our society got to these problems? The truth is: virtually no answer at all. The question of what the

* 'Survival of the Fitter', E F Schumacher, 'The Listener', 1 May 1975.

work does to the worker is hardly ever asked; the proposition that the worker has to adapt himself to the work is hardly ever questioned; and the demand that the work should be adapted to fit the needs of the worker is treated as impractical and utopian . . .

It might be said that it is the ideal of the employer to have production without employees, and the ideal of the employee to have income without work. The question is: can the pursuit of these two ideals, undertaken with the marvellous ingenuity of modern science and technology, lead to anything but total alienation and final breakdown? 'Without work,' said Albert Camus, 'all life goes rotten. But when work is soulless life stifles and dies . . .'

Small is beautiful, and so is simplicity; and so is any efficient technology that can be applied by small and simple people – people without great wealth or great power. The development of our technology has been geared towards such an intensity of capital investment that only people already rich and powerful can really participate; all the others, the vast majority, have been reduced to the position of accessories and gap-fillers. This is a development away from real human needs, and 'managing to survive' must mean bringing things back to real human needs, so that not just a few, but many people, can live independent, self-reliant, productive lives. Do we lack the intelligence to achieve such results? I do not think so. If we do not, at present, achieve the needed result – in terms of a technology with a human face – it is simply for the lack of trying.

What Schumacher is talking about here certainly is political power. Who controls the nature of work? Who decides that it is still proper to use the word 'efficient' to describe a production process that reduces workers to the status of nonentities? We may ask if it is not the duty of designers to do as Schumacher suggests and to design products so that they can be made in a satisfactory way. But then, who is it that decides what it is that designers design? Obviously, it is the same people who, almost without meaning to, are making the decisions that lead to work being the boring drudgery that it so often is. It is only those with economic or political power who have access to the skills that designers can put at their disposal.

A society based on the division of labour is the perfect milieu for the professional. The modern industrial world provides the ideal platform on which the designer can perform as a successful specialist. In such a setting design is naturally aligned with technology and the behavioural sciences. It is seen essentially as an operational means of making changes. The designer appears as an efficient problem solver resolving the world's environmental ills. His context, like that of business or economics or psychiatry, is the busy world of making and doing. The ethics involved are those of intervention and control; of more or less benign paternalism. Certainly a measure of professional detachment is implied. It is not his own problems that the designer is supposed to be solving; they are always somebody else's.

'Benign paternalism.' We can see this characteristic of the designer's role most clearly in the phenomenon of modern public authority housing. At its best, it represents a triumph of humane standards over the philosophy of ruthless commercialism that produced the nineteenth century slums. But it also is the result of a highly organised bureaucracy where designers and clients seldom meet. The result is hard to evaluate. In a recent exhibition, called 'Home Sweet Home', the Greater London Council attempted to provide an honest review of its achievements in the field. Shown here are a number of examples of its work:

Above right
China Walk

Below right
Roehampton Cottages

Far right
Restored terrace, Porchester Square

Above left
Brooklands Park

Above right
Alton West, Roehampton

Left
Roman Way, Andover

Far right above
Swedenborg Square

Far right below
Thamesmead.
(Greater London Council,
Department of Architecture and Civic
Design)

Problems? It is time to look a little more deeply at this word if only because, in the idea of 'problem solving', it has become common usage in design education as well as amongst professional designers. I do not much like the concept because I do not believe that 'problem' and 'solution' really represent the poles between which the designer travels. We have already seen that compromise is inherent in design; any compromise is likely to be only a temporary resting place and it cannot in any sense be said that 'the community' could make such a journey. What we have here is a mechanistic picture of cause and effect (problem/solution) being used as a model for something that is far more subtle, complex and intractable. The effect is to take us into a dangerous world of fantasy.

What we need is something more like an 'ecology' of designing. The use of the concept of a 'solution' implies a moment of stasis before the new way is set. This is not a moment that exists in ecology, and in design it is really only a convenient but confusing fiction. In ecological models we have continuing processes and interactions that never cease acting on each other or stop. The same is true of those systems of which design is a part.

However, it is important to see that the terms on which designers mostly operate tend to reinforce the idea of problem and solution. Designers are usually commissioned to work to a fixed brief where 'the solution' is well known and can be defined. This is generally done either in commercial terms (increased sales) or in terms of a known social model ('build a health centre'). The larger pattern of possibilities and questions ('is it

'*Problems that are never solved.*' *The city presents the design problems of mankind at their most intractable and complex but they would not be swept away if, by some magic wand, cities could be removed from the face of the earth. The same aesthetic, social and political issues would continue to plague us and find expression in design. In any case, it is important to recognise that cities, where we now see only trouble, can also represent freedom and opportunity.*

*As the caption to this '*Picture Post*' photograph of New York says '*They came seeking liberty, prosperity, excitement, peace*'. The same optimism and energy is reflected in the classic film musical '*On the Town*' where three sailors come to New York to enjoy the scale and unique scope that only a great city can give.*
(*'*Picture Post*' from the John Frost collection : Film still from the National Film Archive*)

ethical to increase the sales of this type of product ?' or 'can we redesign the environment so as to stop people getting sick ?') can seldom be brought into the picture.

As a professional – one of Adam Smith's 'very few people' – the designer has invested his future reputation and that of his colleagues in being able to deliver the goods. But, in contemporary conditions, this masks a defect of vision. It makes it very hard indeed for a designer to come to terms with the truth that there are 'problems' that are likely to be 'insoluble' by means of design activity as such. Political activity is what is required. Such a recognition need not necessarily mean that the designer involved has to stop designing ; rather it should make him more honest and realistic. It should greatly increase his humility and his consideration for those who will have to go on living with the buildings or products that are eventually built or made.

It will help to take an example. It is frequently said that planners fail because 'they do not know what people want'. They do not solve people's problems. But most 'bad' designs do not arise because designers are ignorant of what people 'like' or 'need'. They arise because, on a completely different level, one group of people is in conflict with another. What may express itself as a conflict between planners and users is in reality nearly always a conflict between third parties in which *any* solution is to the gain of some and the loss of others. Consider the varying degrees of power wielded by the parties to a redevelopment, and also their varying degrees of access to the

THE PEOPLE UPSTAIRS

The people upstairs all practise ballet.
    Their living room is a bowling alley.
Their bedroom is full of conducted tours.
    Their radio is louder than yours.
They celebrate week ends all the week.
When they take a shower, your ceilings leak.
    They try to get their parties to mix
By supplying their guests with Pogo sticks,
    And when their orgy at last abates,
    They go to the bathroom on roller skates.
I might love the people upstairs wondrous
If instead of above us, they just lived under us.

From 'Versus' copyright 1949 by Ogden Nash

designer whose job it is to find the means to ends that are inevitably incompatible.

In a recent article in *Futures** about the management of conflict, Sir Geoffrey Vickers presented a clear picture of how this works in practice. He described three kinds of disagreements: disagreements about concepts – 'how the situation shall be seen'; disagreements about values – 'how the situation shall be valued'; and disagreements about ways and means – 'how to attain ends'. In this hierarchy it is clear that the designer's freedom of action is usually constrained to being about ways and means rather than about concepts and values. But the debate about concepts and values is the important one. Who are the parties to this debate, what are their interests and how are they expressed? Here is an extract from the article:

It is useful also to distinguish conflictual situations according to what the conflict is about. Three types can be distinguished, though they are always found in combination.

The type least easy to recognise and hardest to resolve involves conflict about what the situation shall be deemed to be.

To a planning authority a decayed urban area is a threat to a number of sanitary and other standards which the authority has a duty to maintain. It is at the same time an opportunity to reshape part of the physical environment to meet more adequately the changed requirements anticipated ten years hence. The two requirements conflict. This conflict, however, is not visible to most of the residents in the area. To them 'the situation' is a variety of current

shortcomings in dwellings and facilities, by no means the same as those which most worry the authority. The criteria which they apply to any proposed change are the benefits promised in terms of these shortcomings and the costs which these would involve in terms of current inconvenience and disturbance. Benefits expected ten years hence have little power to offset costs expected now – and no power at all to do so, unless the residents can learn to attach reality to that view of the situation which is natural to the authority.

An interested developer, on the other hand, has no difficulty in seeing the situation on the same time scale as the planning authority. Even if he sees [it] only as a site ripe for profitable development because of its currently depressed value, it may well be easier for him to understand the situation as seen by the authority and the wider criteria which they apply (even though he does not share these) than it is for those who live in the place.

Even on the authority there will be some councillors who see the situation primarily as the need and opportunity to improve the accommodation of specific ill-housed people, whilst others regard the expected increase in site values as a better criterion of the meeting of foreseen future needs. So differences about what the situation shall be deemed to be express and are affected by differences about the values to be attributed to different criteria of success. And even where agreement exists about the aspects to be included in the situation and about the criteria to apply, fierce differences may still arise about the best course to take. Of the alternative development plans submitted to the authority no legal deductive process can *prove* which is best even by the criteria agreed.

Disagreements about how the situation shall be seen and how it shall be valued are so intimately connected that I find it convenient to describe the two together as differences of appreciation. Conflicts

about how to attain agreed ends, though they bulk so large in studies of decision making, are always subsidiary to appreciative problems and seldom, if ever, raise irresolvable conflicts between those who are at one in their appreciation of a situation.

'Those who are at one in their appreciation of the situation.' In the example given above it is significant that those who are most at one in their appreciation of the situation are also the ones with access to the designer. It is they who will pay him and give him his brief. It is also significant that, in direct human terms, they will not be the people affected most intimately. They will not eventually have to move after having had the experience of living for a large slice of their lives in a steadily deteriorating slum, fatally affected by 'planning blight'. What we are looking at here can not in any sense be described as a 'problem' that the designer could 'solve' by his design. No, the designer, in his design, will inevitably be throwing the weight of his skill onto one side or other of a group of conflicting interests.

Where this kind of intractable social conflict involves design decisions, it is interesting to recognise how very unlike it is to situations found either in science or in most technological design. The differences between them have been well described by Horst Rittel and Melvin Webber† who have given these 'problems of appreciation' a splendidly apt name: they call them 'wicked problems'. Here is an extract

* 'The Management of Conflict', Sir Geoffrey Vickers, 'Futures', Vol 4, No 2, June 1972.

† 'Dilemmas in a general theory of planning', Horst Rittel and Melvin Webber, 'Policy Sciences' 4, 1973.

Those who are most affected by decisions about the environment are frequently the people who have the least power to influence or choose where they will live. For example, a massive slum clearance scheme may mean that children will spend the whole of their most formative years in an area shattered by the process of redevelopment. Such social effects are the often unforeseen results of design approaches intended to achieve the economic benefits that come from large scale operations. They also reflect the conflict of interests which can exist in any rebuilding scheme.
(Chris Ridley)

from what they have to say about them:

The kinds of problems that planners deal with – societal [sic] problems – are inherently different from the problems that scientists and perhaps some classes of engineers deal with. Planning problems are inherently wicked.

As distinguished from problems in the natural sciences, which are definable and separable and may have solutions that are findable, the problems of governmental planning – and especially those of social or policy planning – are ill defined: and they rely on elusive political judgement for resolution. (Not 'solution'. Social problems are never solved. At best they are only re-solved – over and over again.) . . . [On the other hand], The problems that scientists and engineers have usually focused upon are mostly 'tame' or 'benign' ones. As an example, consider a problem of mathematics, such as solving an equation; or the task of an organic chemist in analysing the structure of some unknown compound; or that of the chessplayer attempting to accomplish checkmate in five moves. For each the mission is clear. It is clear, in turn, whether or not the problems have been solved.

They go on to say:

The lay customers are complaining because planners and professionals have not succeeded in solving the problems they claimed they could solve. We shall want to suggest that the social professions were misled somewhere along the line into assuming they could be applied scientists – that they could solve problems in the ways scientists can solve their sorts of problems. The error has been a serious one.

Here is an insight for the teacher of design. The most important design problems are 'wicked' problems of 'appreciation'. They have no clear-cut

The things that people own are a great part of their identity, unique and special to them. Here is a collection of ornaments and mementoes representing the accumulated belongings of an old person. They were assembled as part of an exhibition about the care of infirm and elderly men and women. (King Edward's Hospital Fund for London)

beginning and no clear-cut end; they involve morals and politics as much as technology. And they are too important to be left to professionals such as designers; they are about issues that the community *as a whole* must think out for itself.

Behind these great themes of work and democracy there are others that are less grand in scale but that, nevertheless, dramatically affect the quality of life as it is lived in an industrial society. Many of them are directly related to the nature of mass production.

One of the most obvious problems in a society devoted to change is that people like familiarity. It is a basic and deep feeling. People build up a pattern in their lives that is reflected in all kinds of small ways in their possessions and surroundings. Look at the contents of somebody's pockets and you will know a great deal about them. It is more than a game of amateur detection, for the portable scatter of bits and pieces is genuinely eloquent. Familiarity is too often discounted, or thought of as being solely bound up with the sentimental. Familiarity is more subtle than that, it is part of identity, reassuring and enduring.

Michael Young and Peter Willmott, in their famous book *Family and Kinship in East London,** give a beautiful example of the importance of familiarity in creating a feeling of security and belonging. They describe the difference between a new housing estate and Bethnal Green, and then

* 'Family and Kinship in East London', Michael Young and Peter Willmott, Routledge & Kegan Paul, 1957.

give in a few vivid sentences the reaction of one woman to moving from the old environment to the new:

Instead of the shops of Bethnal Green there is the shopping centre at the Parade; instead of the street barrows piled high with fruit, fish and dresses, instead of the cries of the costermongers from Spitalfields to Old Ford, there are the orderly self-service stores in the marble halls of the great combines. In place of the gaunt buildings rising above narrow streets of narrow houses, there are up-to-date semi-detached residences. Bethnal Green encases the history of three hundred years . . . Greenleigh [the name is imaginary] belongs firmly to the aesthetics of this mid-century . . .

Instead of the hundred, fussy, fading little pubs of the borough there are just the neon lights and armchairs of the Merchant Venturer and the Yeomans Arms. Instead of the barrel organ in Bethnal Green Road there is an electrically amplified musical box in a mechanical ice-cream van. In place of tiny workshops squeezed into a thousand backyards rise the first few glass and concrete factories which will soon give work to Greenleigh's children. Instead of the sociable squash of people and houses, workshops and lorries, there are the drawn-out roads and spacious open ground of the usual low-density estate. Instead of the flat land of East London, the gentle hills of Essex.

'When I first came,' said Mrs Sandeman, 'I cried for weeks, it was so lonely. It was a shock to see such a steep hill going up to the shops.'

This is a good example because it concerns the familiarity of surroundings that have a genuine quality and depth of involvement. It is a good example in another way, too. The force and moving quality of the East End environment comes almost less from what it has done to the

people living there than from what they have done to it. 'Bethnal Green encases the history of three hundred years'; there is no possible substitute for that. A place where buildings that were once houses are now shops, where the furniture workshops down the road were there before the machine age, where families have lived in the same street for a century; this means something in human terms, that is at least as important as the actual aesthetics of those shops, workshops and streets. As with an old chair that has been sat on a very great deal, a certain kind of comfort seems to be vouched for by long use.

At its core this kind of attitude to familiarity and tradition contains the basis of a really fundamental appreciation of environment and everyday objects. To encourage its growth there needs to be respect for people's ability to mould the place in which they live and encouragement for them to do it. But the powerfully tidy minds of bureaucrats and designers combine with 'efficient' production methods to militate against the flexibility, freedom and variety that would help.

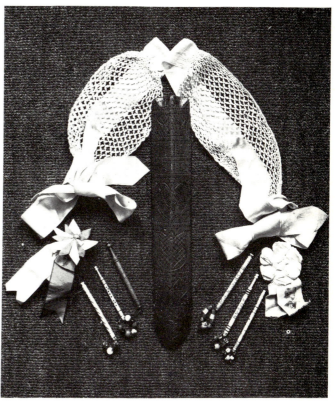

The pictures on the next few pages all show contrasts in quality and feeling.

Above left
Lunch table in the Paris flat of Stephen Gilbert, the sculptor.
(Julian Sheppard)

Above right
Mementoes of love and marriage from the first part of the nineteenth century.
(Hereford and Worcester County Museum, Hartlebury Castle, Kidderminster. Gerald Pates)

Utility living-room in natural waxed oak. Seats of chairs are covered with bright red rexine. Baby's high chair is stained beech. Utility linoleum covers the floor. The lunch is served in utility china, and will be eaten with utility forks and knives. Father wears his best utility suit (eight pockets, plain trousers, cost £4 9s. 6d.). Mother wears her blue wool dress (£3 os. od.). The little boy's outfit can be bought for £1 os. od. and is from top to toe. Baby's rompers cost 11s. 5d. Clothes by Simpsons, Pica

PREVIEW OF A UTILITY HOME

The utility family relaxes. Father is displaying his shirt (10s. 9d.) socks (2s. 9d.) and black boxcalf shoes (36s.), all utility. Mother is wearing her utility stockings (3s. 8d.). Toys are not utility

On January 1 utility furniture will be available to those who can prove they need it. Here **ILLUSTRATED** shows something of the utility life of 1943

Father and son sit on a utility bed-settee covered with cot damask. Book-shelf and woodwork of bed-settee are stained b

Another quality that people almost always appreciate is workmanship. This, too, is related to familiarity, because workmanship is a part of durability and therefore a token of an object's continuing existence. Of all the problems resulting from the Industrial Revolution and the contemporary world's dependence on mass production, the ambiguity of machine-made workmanship looks like being one of the most persistent. The fact that there is a relentless relationship between price and volume of sales can mean that mass-produced goods are deliberately made not to last, but even apart from that, the actual character of inexpensive machine-made objects is not naturally eloquent of the generally accepted symbols of workmanship. This is hardly surprising, because workmanship implies time spent and effort expended, while the whole point of mass production is to make more in less time and with less effort.

Left, above and right
An issue of 'Illustrated' dealing with the excellent quantity-produced utility furniture that was designed and produced during the Second World War. ('Illustrated' from the John Frost collection)

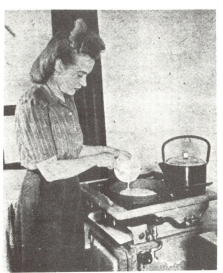

Right
Advertisement for a mass-produced plastic kitchen rubbish bin. Read the copy below, see how it appeals to the popular feeling for natural materials, craftsmanship and the need for unique things!
(Peter Jones)

'*Most people will think it was carved by an old world cabinetmaker . . . What Brentwood does for garbage cans, Brentwood also does for matching towel dispensers, bread boxes, canister sets, hampers, ice buckets, waste baskets, and many other household items. All available in four distinctive finishes. Oak, Walnut, Moss Green and Antique White. The Brentwood Step-on Can costs only $15.95. You'll never have to hide the garbage can under the sink again.*'

Far right
The standardised façade of a block of flats. Flowers and curtains : a strict convention with which individuality struggles heroically to assert itself.
(Chris Ridley)

THE GARBAGE CAN

Most people will think it was carved by an old world cabinetmaker.
Brentwood hand-rubs the finish to create a custom look. Made of incredible Duralene™ that never needs polishing. Shrugs off stains and scratches. Cleans with a damp cloth.
We've made other improvements, too. A step-on hinge that doesn't catch the way others do. (Our lab people haven't been able to wear it out yet.) An unbreakable, removable liner. And a deodorizer in the lid.
What Brentwood does for garbage cans, Brentwood also does for matching towel dispensers, bread boxes, canister sets, hampers, ice buckets, waste baskets, and many other household items. All available in four distinctive finishes. Oak, Walnut, Moss Green and Antique White.
The Brentwood Step-On Can costs only $15.95*. You'll never have to hide the garbage can under the sink again.

BRENTWOOD
Puts an end to the Uglies

Looking back on the history of the Industrial Revolution it is clear that, consciously or not, the early manufacturers recoiled from the problem. Machinery was used to give a spurious impression of workmanship – of time and effort spent where in fact it had not been spent. The technique grew to maturity living on a lie. The great absurdity is that industry ever set out to give mass-produced goods an ersatz quality of workmanship; the tragedy is that because the trick was tried out the real issues have been hopelessly confused, at least for the vast majority of people who simply want to enjoy the cheap goods they can buy in the shops.

Economic pressures have had a similar effect on buildings. Anyone with a real feeling for workmanship could be reduced almost to tears by the wood and brickwork on a contemporary housing estate. Time and cost dictate the use of desperately skimped standards. The people who live in the resulting houses accept what they can get, but acceptance does not mean that they are satisfied. The millions of people who visit old houses and 'beauty spots' every year are hungry for qualities that do not exist in their own everyday lives.

This is not to say that mass-produced goods are inevitably badly made. They are not. The point here is to try to make clear why it is very difficult for goods made in this way to satisfy people's appreciation for workmanship, and to suggest that this has become a surprisingly intractable problem leading to genuine dissatisfaction.

The problem of stability and the problem of workmanship are primarily cultural and aesthetic. But

there is also a vast problem about the more directly practical issue of function. In terms of mass production, this is related to workmanship but involves a variety of other difficulties as well. People want equipment to work. They expect houses, schools and shops to keep the weather out, to contain the activities they were built to house, and to last long enough to minimise the costs of repair. They expect domestic appliances and a great many other products to help them to lead lives with less routine drudgery. That they are sometimes disappointed in these hopes is demonstrated simply enough by the existence of the Consumers' Association and the Design Council, but the depth of their disillusionment is to be found as vehemently expressed in other places.

It is easy to trace, in films, in literature and in the conversation of people on the Underground, the murmur of this particular discontent. The inefficient functioning of objects and buildings has even produced its own distinctive humour, and the persecution of Thurber by his motorcar stands as the prototype of a whole literature of bursting water heaters and recalcitrant lawn-mowers. Thurber understood terribly well the awful paradox of hope and disillusionment that besets technological man in his encounters with the environment. We are Walter Mitty, heroic in the mechanised air battle, but we are also Thurber's father yelling 'God Almighty' when he thinks the motor has dropped out of his car.

Much the same ambivalence of feeling lies behind our liking for the moments of destruction in

*Windows and archway in old buildings in Wisbech.
(Design Council)*

The battle with objects. People expect things to work and help them to lead a more comfortable life. It doesn't always happen and a lot of twentieth century comedy is based on this sad fact. In the illustration Weary Willie and Tired Tim cause havoc in a garage forecourt but triumph in the end. This issue of 'Chips' is dated 1947.
(Syndication International Ltd)

Many design problems result from conflicts of interest between groups of people. This may be a matter of exploitation : it may be a matter of straightforward human cussedness .

entertainment when man is revenged on his possessions. It is difficult to see how this kind of thing could have seemed funny before the nineteenth century, but now the sight of Laurel and Hardy systematically and slowly breaking up a house is one of the most wonderful and hilarious episodes imaginable. It is so right, so perfectly just. And in a more subtle way Jacques Tati, blundering through the awful modernity of suburbia in his film *Mon Oncle*, is a justified wrecker restoring the balance in favour of man. When he finally makes the polythene pipe machine in the clinical factory get hiccoughs and belch out senseless lengths of plastic sausages, we feel it is a great moral victory that the machine has been made to look an idiot. It is funny because we all so often seem to experience the situation in reverse.

It is a cliché to say that this is a materialist period, and it is certainly true that since the Industrial Revolution men have developed the world of things to an unprecedented degree. It is also true that in some senses men now live *through* their possessions more than ever before, but it is important to realise that this is an extension of something that has always happened, something not necessarily bad in itself. Venice, if you look at it one way, is the most riotous expression of out-and-out materialism in Europe, but the patronage of the merchant princes resulted in a piece of environment that is timeless in its relevance to the human scale and the poetry of human life.

What is distinctive about the present is that industrialisation has made possible the extension of patronage almost throughout society. Whereas the main character of the environment in the past was largely determined by a small group of rich men whose taste permeated downwards, today it is determined by the mass of the community. But it is a patronage exercised without the sense of actually being a patron; a plenty soured by exploitation and helpless anonymity. You don't feel much of a patron when the refrigerator you buy is exactly the same as Mrs Brown's down the road. You don't feel much of a patron when the character of the house you live in is largely the result of standardised decisions taken either in a council office or in a property company's design department.

In a way which Adam Smith did not foresee, the community has paid a complex cultural price for the wealth produced by mass production and the division of labour.

So far this chapter has dealt with discontent. And there is discontent, widespread and bitter. It exists in the design professions themselves as well as in society at large. This must be hopeful. It is remarkable that the designer and the community should react in the same way at the same time. It is not something that happened when the pioneers of modern design were working out their programmes. Then they *knew* and the public *didn't*. Now both are full of doubts. On such a basis progress might be made. Specialist 'designers' and non-specialist 'users' might be able to move closer together and, in the process, transform both the nature of designing and the alienating effects of industrialisation and bureaucratic management.

Out of the present confusion it looks possible to predict two major interrelated changes of emphasis in design. The first will be a move away from the *designer* as the major focus of interest. Instead the emphasis will be thrown back on the *community*, and the ways in which political and economic decisions determine a large part of the character and functioning of the environment. The second change will be away from the analysis of design in terms of the appreciation of solutions. The realisation of the community's central role is going to require people's involvement, not as passive appreciators of 'truth and beauty', but as active participants in making decisions.

Although it is easy to understand why it happened, it is disastrous that practically all the officially supported efforts to educate the public in design since 1951 have concentrated on achieving *acceptance*, not *discussion*. People have been presented with a credo about aesthetic taste, not an analysis of the difficulties inherent in meeting men's needs by mass production. But if, as Christopher Jones says, '. . . design decisions ought to become less the responsibility of consumers', then the real debate will have to begin.

Marcel Duchamp, the French artist who was one of the founders of the Dadaist movement and a sharp critic of accepted ideas about painting, had a theory that the onlooker is as important as the artist. He said that what society chooses to take from a work of art is the really important part, even though it may not be what the artist originally intended. 'The onlooker is as important as the artist. In spite of what the artist thinks he is doing, something stays on that is completely independent of what he intended, and that something is grabbed by society – if he's lucky. The artist himself doesn't count. Society just takes what it wants. The work of art is always based on these two poles of the maker and the onlooker, and the spark that comes from this bi-polar action gives birth to something, like electricity.'

Something similar has, in the past, been true of design. It has been the designer's job deliberately to make the spark jump, but it has proved a chancy business at best. What we are now feeling our way towards is a less passive role for the 'onlooker', and a less dangerously haphazard way of generating the necessary electricity.

My own belief is that design education has a key role to play in this development. This is not only because it will 'educate' the public, but because it will provide the workshop in which new ways of designing – accessible and not esoteric ones – will be created.

'Society in its full sense,' wrote Ruth Benedict in 1935, 'is never entirely separable from the individuals who compose it. No individual can arrive at the threshold of his potentialities without a culture in which he participates. Conversely, no civilisation has in it any element which in the last analysis is not the contribution of an individual.' This general statement is today of great importance for the future development of design and design education. The relationship between people and culture, which in industrial society has partly broken down, can only be rebuilt painfully. But both our particular elements – the designer and education – must move closer together if the modern world is to achieve its staggering potential to the full. The designer must become more expert in understanding people's needs, but it is also vital that there should be more widespread appreciation of the designer's problems and of the way his solutions can be carried out by industry. And the community must accept greater responsibility for those design 'problems' that are really the result of its own inner conflicts.

Changes in educational theory and practice are to be expected. It is not, at the moment, at all clear that we are seriously educating children to take an active place in a genuinely democratic society. We give them a lot of practice in absorbing knowledge; little in reasoning or decision making; hardly any in handling problems of appreciation. The world of children at school is made up of 'benign' problems and the ethic of the classroom is still to know the answer. Wicked problems, which call for an understanding of nonconformity and the expression of moral and ethical diversity, are the antithesis of what is generally talked about by teachers and children. Not to know the definitive and socially accepted answer is, in most schools, to be branded at best a failure and at worst a trouble maker.

But, again, there *are* signs of substantial change. In 1974 there was an important conference at Horncastle organised by the Department of Education and Science. One of the speakers was Philip Roberts, schoolteacher secretary of the National Association for Design Education. In his contribution he attempted to sum up the present scope of design education in schools and to look to the future. Here is something of what he had to say:

A natural result of looking at social needs and design problems (instead of preconceived solutions) is to make design studies educationally more valid, and socially aware and responsive. In some cases there has been a move towards a greater consideration of *systems*, with discussion of the relation between parts of the system, and their social implications. For instance, instead of starting with the idea of making a car, the start is made with the idea of a transport system into which components must fit. This naturally brings into focus such issues as pollution, the depletion of resources and the value of the individual and society in relation to technology, economics, fashion and so on. This kind of analysis, which really should be the essence of design education, could alter radically the nature of education in relation to society: in its implications, this genuinely *is* a revolutionary approach.

The next step in design education is obvious and reasonable but it has not yet been defined by secondary teachers in practical and explicit teaching terms. What is needed in the future is design education at the level of the whole community leading to the participation by one and all in environmental decisions. In the majority of cases a social and political structure for design education in this broad sense has not been considered, though it is hinted at in some syllabuses which are based on man and his environment.

A social balance sheet that weighs the advantages and disadvantages of mass production fairly is very difficult to draw up. Our whole way of living now depends on industrialisation, and mass production is the essential element that allows the Western world to support its enormously increased population. But if, as is certain, urban society today contains a completely unprecedented range of possibilities for the development of ordinary people, it is also true that certain aspects of life have been impoverished along the way. The sympathy and understanding that used to exist between the craftsman, the things he made and the people who used them, were destroyed, and we are only now beginning to see what might satisfactorily be put in their place.

In one sense the designer and the teacher of design are trying to re-establish, on a new basis related to modern conditions, the close link that the craftsman naturally had with the people who used the things he made. It is an extraordinarily difficult thing to do and, so far, there have been more failures than successes. But the movement in a new direction is strongly under way. Significantly, liberal, democratic ideals point to identical developments in design and education. The end result could be a dramatic release of creative energy in school, at work and in the environment.

Chapter 4

Design in education

In this chapter I intend to ignore all those formidable problems of detailed organisation and curriculum planning that I mentioned briefly in Chapter 1, even though I know that they still plague teachers in their everyday work in schools and are likely to go on doing so for the foreseeable future. I shall not mention the interrelationships between various school subjects such as art, home economics, environmental studies, and woodwork and metalwork, even though I know that they form a large part of the practical difficulties afflicting design departments and faculties. I shall not look at such explosive and emotive issues as the importance of teaching craft skills, the real nature of home economics or the proper balance between, for example, design and materials science in an examination called 'Design and Technology', even though I know that it is these problems of content that are debated fiercely wherever teachers get together to discuss 'design'.

These omissions are quite deliberate. There are two reasons for them. The first, and most obvious, is that the issues are dealt with at some length in the Royal College of Art study to which I have contributed. But this is not the most important reason. The second is the one that really counts; it is to do with the nature and purpose of the present book and its relationship to current educational problems in the field of design.

I argued in the introduction that, at the moment, the main difficulty facing teachers in design education comes from a confusion about the central concept of design itself. The majority of the specific problems just mentioned stem directly from misconceptions about either the scope or the nature of design. In reality, the problems are not about design at all. Instead, they are the result of the strains of transition: they come from the struggle involved in adapting a group of existing subject traditions to the growing recognition that design activity has much to offer as a medium for education.

I do not believe that we are as yet in a position to predict in a precise way the outcome of a better understanding of the central concept. That will, in any case, be a matter for the specialist teachers involved. It is work for the future.

Against such a background, it seems most useful simply to attempt to state clearly the special characteristics and opportunities that the study of design has to offer in general education in the future. A recognition of these characteristics and opportunities does not imply faith in any particular form of school organisation, balance of content or subject specialisation. It does however imply the belief that teachers need a better base for future planning and for understanding the potential of design activity. The present chapter is an attempt to describe where that potential lies and what is its essential nature.

So far, the main emphasis of this book has been what might be called 'instrumental'. Although I have tried to point out the social, historical and economic perspectives, because I believe they are important, buildings and products have nonetheless held the centre of the stage. It is a concern with these particular expressions of mankind's creativity that defines design as a unique discipline distinct from, say, literature or science. But when we turn to general education, the emphasis must change. We find ourselves looking, instead, at the growth and development of children and young people: at their journey from childhood to participation in a full and mature adult life. We find ourselves looking at design activity mainly from the standpoint of the contribution it can make to the personal development of individuals in society.

There is a traditional maxim among woodwork teachers who say: 'It is not the effect of the boy on the wood that interests us, it is the effect of the wood on the boy.' Here is the appropriate emphasis in a nutshell. We ought to recognise, however, that we are not dealing with a conflict between the 'inner' and 'outer' aspects of design activity and awareness. The special characteristic of design and related experiences in art and craft is that they carry the inner world of values into the intractable outer world of natural resources. We could say that the aim of design education is to make it

possible for the child to develop his own innate capacities to the point where he is fully able to enjoy the experiences, knowledge and skills that men have created for using, dealing with, understanding and valuing this natural environment. What we are talking about is a *personal* development which has the idea of cultural *participation* as one of its main ingredients.

But what, in practice, does this mean? How can such ideals find realistic expression in the classroom?

As long ago as 1967, when Kate and I were looking at design education in Leicestershire, it was already possible to write appreciatively of what could be seen. Under the headings 'Teaching Design' and 'Housecraft Teaching', we wrote the following:*

Teaching design
Nearly every teacher we spoke to felt that design should play a more important part in handicraft teaching than used to be the case. To many, it is beginning to appear the one activity capable of holding together the different directions in wood and metalwork, while at the same time making sense of workmanship in an industrial community.

In Leicestershire, any boy taking handicraft would be introduced to the idea of industrial design, though with varying degrees of success. The least valid pieces of teaching were those that concentrated on taste; the best involved a realistic consideration of design in all its complexity as a functional-cum-aesthetic problem

* *'Classroom consumers – the moulding of a design public', Ken and Kate Baynes, 'Design' magazine No 217. January 1967.*

related to available means of construction and materials. It is worth looking in more detail at two specific examples.

At the Humphrey Perkins school in Barrow-on-Soar we saw children working on the design and construction of a metal legged stool. Brian Crump, the handicraft teacher, had introduced the ergonomics of the subject through magazine photographs of various bottoms on seats (which the children enjoyed) and then sent them home to measure up Mum and Dad. They got some incredible results! Each child then interpreted what it had learned in a design which was also related to a certain amount of knowledge about what could be done in metalwork. At this stage the development of the design became a matter of individual tuition, with Mr Crump steering a delicate path between encouraging inventiveness and setting limits which would allow a finished stool to be made successfully.

When we visited the school, the boys had started construction work, and it was obvious that the whole project had aroused their enthusiasm in a way that simply learning the techniques of metalwork often fails to do. The element of entertainment involved in taking Mum and Dad's vital statistics should not be underestimated as just a joke – it is exactly the kind of link with the everyday that is disastrously lacking in bad art and craft teaching.

We saw a completely different kind of valid design activity at Market Harborough Grammar School where the head of the handicraft department, Geoff Gorman, was particularly concerned to make effective links with

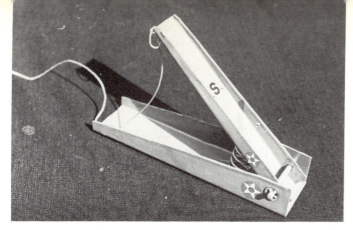

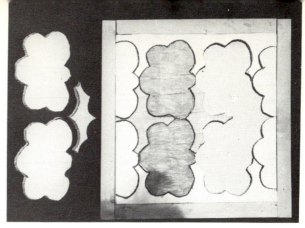

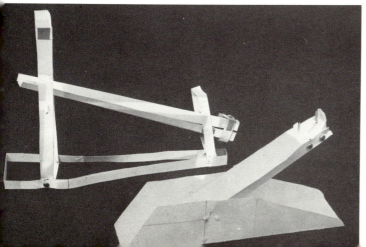

This page – first year projects

At Pocklington School in Yorkshire the approach to design work in the first years of secondary education is to attempt to broaden the experience of the children and to encourage their ability to use drawing and other visual media as a way of understanding the world and communicating about it.

Shown here is a selection of the work done on the course.

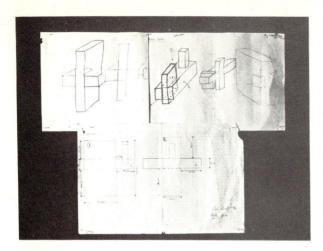

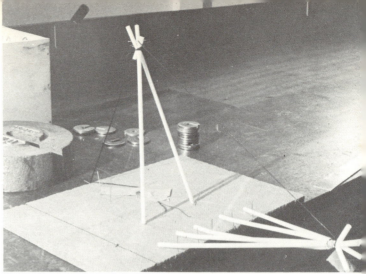

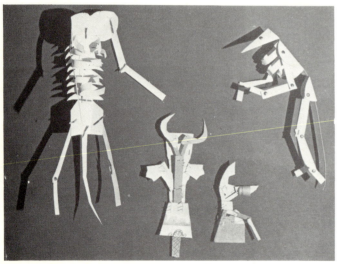

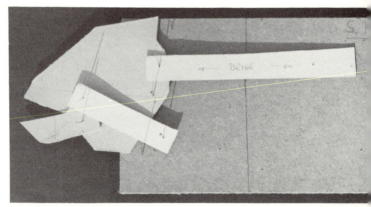

*Pocklington School third year projects
In a note on their course, the teachers in
charge, R N Billington and J R Jeffrey,
say this : 'The first requirement in the
development of design awareness is a
strong emphasis on the knowledge and
understanding achieved through the
study and analysis of natural and
man-made forms which stimulate both
the intellect and the imagination. The
child discovers through these exercises
how things look, feel, work and behave.*

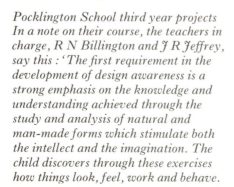

science and engineering. Here boys studying science use their handicraft periods to design and make experimental apparatus.

Mr Gorman showed us a number of devices which had been made to demonstrate expansion in metal, and the result of a group project to make a rig which would measure the coefficient of friction between a cycle wheel rim and a brake block. The great virtue of what was being done was that craftsmanship was being used for a specific experimental purpose, involving the fitting together of intellectual concepts with practical methods of construction. These two examples show clearly the potential of the wood and metal workshops in design education. But it seems to us that what we were seeing was the start of something rather than the conclusion . . .

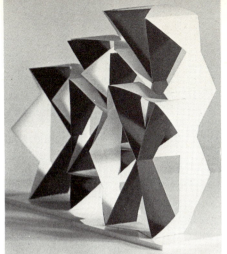

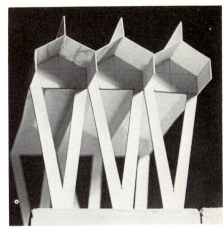

Where a school has a design education programme that runs through the whole of each child's school career, the variety of work that can be achieved is very large. The examples shown here are from Ravens Wood School in Bromley where Owen Frampton is in charge of art and design studies.

'New Shapes', a theme studied in the second, third and fourth years.

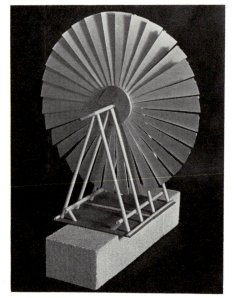

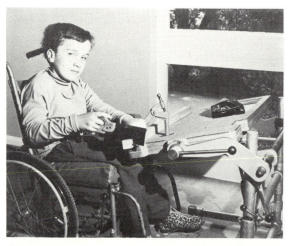

Ravens Wood School

*Top right, top left and above
The results of a third year project that
was concerned with the construction of
wind machines.*

*Right and above right
A major design project. A workbench
for spina bifida children designed and
developed by John Fry, a senior pupil at
the school.*

Clothes are frequently used in schools as a basis for design work. They present demanding problems and involve a consideration of structure and human proportions as well as craftsmanship and social and aesthetic questions such as fashion and colour . . . they are also fun!

Right
Dress shown at the exhibition held to coincide with the Royal College of Art Summer School in 1975.

Below right
Design for a shoe-sandal made as part of a joint art/woodwork project in a secondary school. (Peter Green/ Middlesex Polytechnic)

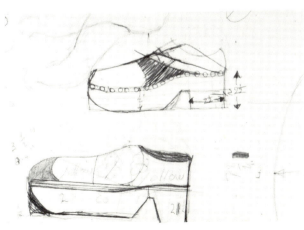

Housecraft teaching

Some of the most immediately effective design teaching in Leicestershire goes on in housecraft departments. Design and choice here are becoming an integral part of the girls' [and boys'] education in running a home and dressing well.

Because the subject is seen in relation to topics which fundamentally interest the children and seem 'adult', it naturally has some inherent sticking power. The rows of electric and gas cookers – each one different – hired from the local gas and electricity boards, give the basis of a miniature *Which?* test, and a foolproof exercise in discrimination. 'I wouldn't want to cook on that one, it's horrible to clean', is a comment based on experience that will not be forgotten. Above all, the link between everyday life and design is seen as quite evidently real. In the same way, work on dressmaking provides an introduction to colour, form and texture in a context which needs no tricks to make it interesting to the majority of children. At Hinckley Grammar School, Miss Stafford, the head of the housecraft department, showed us a selection of dresses some of which were surprisingly sophisticated and intelligent in their selection of fabrics. Nearly all were of a very high standard of workmanship. She also showed us some impressive notebooks which girls had prepared as part of their Certificate of Secondary Education (CSE) examination work. In the best of these, the girls' experience of dressmaking by hand was carried over into an understanding of the qualities and limitations of mass-produced clothes.

All housecraft departments in Leicestershire contain either a miniature flat or a room where the pupils can occasionally entertain friends, parents or staff. They are carefully furnished and equipped within the limitations of the county's budget, and provide some experience of well designed objects brought together in a convincing simulation of a domestic setting. The interiors are not static. The pupils add to them themselves, making curtains, toys and chair covers, and in one school, working with the art department, they had repainted the room to an excellent scheme of their own . . .

A great deal of this kind of work is now done in schools. It has almost become commonplace. But that should not blind us to its underlying values and their significance. In each example can be glimpsed the beginnings of an attempt to encompass the open-ended, exploratory, questioning aspects of design while relating them, at the same time, to an awareness of such things as human needs, style, materials and technology. We can recognise, too, an emphasis on the priority that, in education, must be overriding: all the teachers we spoke to were primarily concerned with the development of their pupils as people and saw design activity as providing special opportunities in this respect.

Since 1967 there have been a number of attempts to give greater substance to this movement towards design activity in schools. The general direction has been rather similar whatever the particular orientation of the teachers or researchers involved. Both *Project Technology* and the Keele project, organised under the auspices of the Schools Council, emphasised the importance of children learning about design by means of designing, and the 8 to 13 project at Goldsmith's College concentrated on observing how children actually did develop in a variety of creative situations. The

Ravens Wood School

Above
'Box rooms' designed and made in the second year.

Below
Desk trays in the sixth form.

majority of the most promising new CSE syllabuses involve the child in open-ended project work and, altogether, there has been a general recognition that introducing design into the classroom means a fundamental change in the relationship between the learner and the teacher. The diversity of design activity means that both will be travelling together in an exploration of the unknown, instead of the teacher being the one who knows the way because he has been there before.

Once again, it is helpful to see how this works out in practice, because the implications can be quite complex. Clearly the necessary approaches may conflict with traditional procedures in art and craft education as well as with those in more 'academic' subjects. What we need to do here is to recognise what is positive and creative in the new developments. I give in the following pages three extended examples of the concepts involved and the kinds of arguments that have been employed by those actively engaged in the field. The first example is an extract from a paper by Malcolm Deere on the new Oxford A-level examination in design for which he is the chief examiner. The second is a 'personal statement' of my own prepared for one of a series of discussion meetings between architects and teachers held during the planning of the Front Door project at Pimlico School. The third is a paper on the idea of problem solving by two experienced teachers: Philip Roberts and John Harahan. Taken together, they should give something of the flavour of design activity when it is seen as an essential element in general education.

A number of schools in Britain are successful in tackling sophisticated work in engineering design, particularly at fifth and sixth form level. Shown here are examples from Whitby County Comprehensive School in Cheshire. The recovery bed was developed in conjunction with a hospital and is now in use there. The mounting for a Newton telescope was made as part of a sixth form course in 'the Elements of Engineering'. The work was done under the guidance of Paul Haskew.

Example 1

The Oxford A-level examination in
Design*
Malcolm Deere

Clearly, not all proposals affecting
design in general education will
include an examination, nor should
they. However, I make no apology for
discussing examination problems,
since, in the abstract, to *consider* an
examination and all its mechanism is
to confront one's aims and objectives,
and it is *these* that are important. Put
another way, the problems of
examining design are the problems of
developing design education itself,
and it is some of these problems that
I wish to examine.

Intentions and strategies

It is not easy to reduce the original
intentions of those who planned the
examination to a simple statement
without distorting what actually took
place. I believe that it is fair to say that
there were three broad principles: to
achieve a solid foundation by setting
up an Advanced level GCE
examination; to cater for a broad view
of design, rather than one that
restricted the activity to a narrow
area; to inculcate both a breadth of
awareness of design, *and* a depth of
specialism – the latter relating
strongly to the field of materials and
processes.

These intentions were translated
into strategy by providing for a
two-part examination, consisting of
two written, orthodox papers,
together with an assessment of a range

of practical work, including an
individual, in-depth, design study.
Interestingly, the two components
closely correspond to the 'design
awareness' and 'design activity'
mentioned in some of the RCA
papers. The 'marks' gained were to be
shared between the two components,
the novelty being that the *bigger*
fraction went to the 'activity' rather
than the examination. The Oxford
Board deserves much thanks for its
courage in sponsoring what, at
Advanced level, is a novel
arrangement; it also involved
acceptance of the practical
assessment being based on both
school marking, and close personal
involvement by a visiting examiner.

Some conflicts and their resolution

Let me now list what I see as the
immediate problems of a design
examination at A-level: they all
represent conflict in some form.

1 School design versus 'Real' design.
2 'Thinking about Design' versus 'Designing'.
3 'Being interested in design' versus 'having innate flair as a designer'.
4 'Design as Technology' versus 'Design as Aesthetics'.
5 'Teaching Design' versus 'Examining Design'.

Having set down five conflict areas,
it will I think be obvious that they
interact. I certainly found as examiner
that I had to consider them all
together, and it is because of this that I
propose to discuss them
collectively. I shall do this by
proposing examination principles.
The first of these is that
examinations should follow and

reflect teaching, they should avoid
moulding it, constraining it, or
stereotyping it. Of course, it would be
silly to deny that this has not
happened on occasion. It requires a
continuous vigilance to minimise it,
and this is best achieved by close
contact with teachers. I see it as the
biggest danger that examinations can
present to design education. The cure
is to present syllabus material as
broad conceptual structures, and to
formulate the right type of question.

The questions are intended to
respect the enthusiasms and interests
of individual teachers (and therefore
their students) by allowing and
encouraging answers that give
'internal choice'; that can include
examples from the individual's own
experience (and thereby encourage
local observation and local
considerations); that make individual
opinions – however unusual – valid, as
long as they are justified in the
candidate's own terms. In sum, we
seek to respect the individual outlook.
What we do *not* do is to require
designing away from source material
and against the clock, because real
design is not like that. Thus, rather
than ask someone to design
something, we ask them what they
would consider to be important *if* they
designed it.

Then, again, we positively allow
specialisation, through the structure
of the paper itself. We want both a
narrow knowledge in depth, *and* a
broader shallower background. Thus,
in the section on materials, we could
well ask the candidate as the
'specialist' to compare his 'formal'
knowledge of steel with what he
conjectures to be the properties of
plastics. Lastly, we encourage

* This is an extract from a paper given at the
Royal College of Art Summer School, 1975.

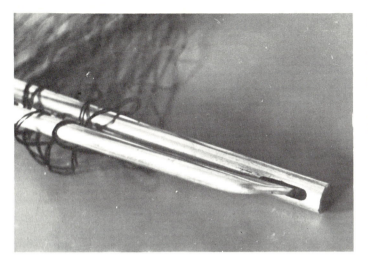

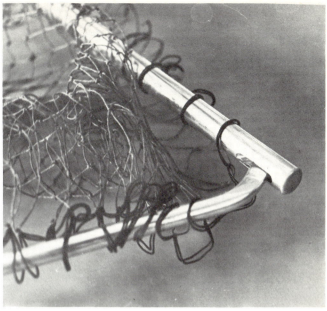

Examples of the very high level of design ability that is achieved by candidates for the Oxford A-level examinations. These projects are from the Nantwich and Acton Grammar School in Cheshire where Mr P Roberts is head of craft.

A landing net designed and developed by 17 year old Ian Brookes.

background reading, but not on the 'set book' principle. The questions are framed so that the answer can make topical reference to events or products occurring the week before the examination.

Turning to the practical work, the major exercise takes nearly a year, and seeks to integrate a wide spectrum of activity and outlook within a single individually selected task. Two aspects seem vital: that all concerned know the qualities that are being sought beforehand (these are listed as a part of the assessment sheet reproduced on pages 118 and 119); and that the 'product' is not only seen in professional terms, but that it is also assessed on the way the student

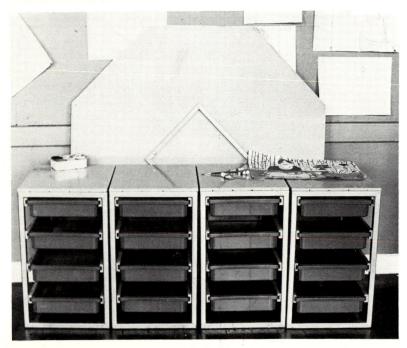

Oxford A-level work from Nantwich and Acton Grammar School.

A storage unit designed and developed by 17 year old Andrew Knonks.

justifies his actions, and subsequently evaluates them. It may seem curious, but we are able to cater for a wide range of tasks within the same framework; largely, I think, because the assessment sheet is not an end in itself, but an aid by which teacher and examiner move towards a jointly awarded grade.

We seek also to complement the main task with a range of activities. In that these develop basic skills, they are necessary precursors to the main task. However, they also provide contrast. For example, we encourage individuals to explore in order to discover, as well as to create functional products. They are encouraged to criticise existing products as well as to conceive new ones; in this way, we sharpen observation and develop the holding and defending of aesthetic and other opinions. This supporting area is much more difficult to assess, and our remedy is to assess it 'coarsely' and with reasonable generosity.

In the light of this discussion, I would say that the five conflicts listed above are real enough, and they require a lot of work if they are to be contained. I doubt if we will ever solve them but I do believe that they can be tamed a little. Indeed, their continuing existence is probably the factor that maintains a very necessary tension, because, after all, design is the pursuit of problems, fascinating in their variety and very uninteresting when they are really dead. I believe that the existence of a design examination is a necessary element in developing design education. It gives an element of discipline and credibility to the whole field, supporting other, equally important

ventures. The essential requirement is that we explore carefully and continuously what sort of examination we want, what we require of it, and what it really gives us.

Lessons for the educational system

As I near the end, I may begin to appear to be bitter. This is not my intention. I want to be clearly understood – I feel that I am representing a group of teachers of worth, and a larger group of their students of great potential. Their participation – pioneering as it has been – represents courage, because there has been much at risk. Between us we have learned some important lessons, which I feel I must now relate.

First, it seems necessary to assert that, in the field of design, Leicestershire – where this enterprise began – is no better than and no worse than many other authorities. It is harmful to the authority, and to the discipline, if one authority is artificially and extravagantly held up as a paragon. Visitors see the part and equate it to the whole, often applying criteria which they associate with the whole by a sort of summative process, arriving at a conclusion which may be far removed from the vision of the individual school. As in politics, so in education the cult of the 'individual' can be dangerous. Next, the educational 'establishment' – meaning bodies like the Schools Council, to take but one example – can fall into a similar trap. They sample a part, and assume it to represent the whole. I believe in accountability: it seems right – it is even helpful and stimulating – to face

the requirement whereby developments such as ours are inspected by a higher authority from time to time. I am, however, at a loss to understand how conclusions can be drawn from the examination scripts without inspecting the 'practical' work as well. I do not want to be too specific, because – to me at least – a common more general problem has emerged. If a new development is to be accepted, or even tolerated, it has to be made to fit by moulding it into a traditional image. Subsequently, it is judged by that moulding alone. My concern is that the real value is thereby missed, and this leads me to my third lesson.

This third conclusion is the strongest of all. Time and again teachers have told me that the success of the course is not so much in the development of design awareness or design expertise, as in the quality of the people that it produces as individuals. One realises when interviewing candidates just what mature, rounded, *whole* people they are. I have not found this to the same extent in any other area of the curriculum. This reflects, in part, I think, a very important feature. It is the very fruitful teaching relationship that is apparent in design education. It is an approach based on the teacher learning *with* his students, on recognition of fallibility, on a kind of mutual respect. This, too, is not seen elsewhere; our task is to develop it, to improve it, above all to preserve it . . .

I am convinced that this is the aspect that most strongly justifies the place of design in general education – its potential contribution is quite unique.

A83 DESIGN (Assessment form A)	PROJECT ASSESSMENT Project Title:		
Heading	RATING Tick one box per row		
Comprehension of project as a whole?	No significant omissions	Project considered in very wide context	Adequate scope of relevant factors
Identification of need for information?	All necessary areas recognised	Most facets of project were considered	Showed adequate foresight
Thoroughness in gaining information: by experiment etc.	Experiments thoroughly exploited	Experiments etc. competently performed	Experiments performed adequately
Ditto: by search and consultation?	Widest possible range of sources explored	Several types of source extensively searched	Reasonable coverage achieved
Decisions intelligently based on available evidence?	Available evidence carefully weighed	Considerable logical deduction was used	Reasonable amount of thought given
Consideration of several possible solutions?	Range of possibilities identified and explored	Several other possibilities properly considered	At least one alternative considered
Planning and organisation of work	Tight control on current target	Intelligent changes of target as circumstances changed	Reasonable ability to manage time and effort
How well was project chosen (considering resources and need)?	Saw real need which could be achieved	Sound target based on slight deficiency in recognising resources or vice versa	Reasonable need based on adequate recognition of resources
Quality of manufacture and assembly – having regard to demands of project?	Own limitations and demands of design well recognised	Good overall, but with slight deficiencies	Adequate degree of skill achieved
Completeness of report?	Very complete and detailed record	All aspects covered, but in variable depth	Rather patchy
How well does report justify project and evaluation?	Covers underlying thinking completely	Very revealing about underlying thinking	Good in some areas
How well is the report itself designed?	Well organised and most competently made	Shows attention to detail, and thought in its layout	Adequate, but not striking in any respect
How well and aptly has the candidate illustrated ideas?	Well-chosen, varied illustration; fair level of skill	Fair level of skill, some reservation on variety or aptness	Adequately chosen and reasonably executed
How well was project evaluated (on own actions)?	Comprehensive review of own actions	Very fair review of own actions	Reasonable or adequate second view of *some* actions
How well was project evaluated (with reference to design process)?	Able to give good criticism dispassionately	A good criticism with a few 'blind-spots'	Recognises some significant reasons for redesign
Natural flair for, and sensitivity to, design?	A natural fluent and sensitive designer	Markedly good in this respect	Average in this respect
Where would you place this project?	Top 10%	Top 25%	In the middle

SCHOOL		CANDIDATE		TUTOR
		Teacher Involvement		**JUSTIFICATION**
		Which heading needed *most* help?	Which heading needed *least* help?	Where appropriate refer to the report; the 'product'; log book; notes, or sketches; tutor's impression; any other factors.
Few additional factors outside immediate target	Very limited view indeed			
Only limited need for information recognised	Saw no need for any information			
Only rather trivial tests performed	No tests worthy of the name			
Some information was acquired	No real sources consulted			
Some thought was given to evidence	Decisions taken on random basis			
Existence of other possibilities recognised	No other possibilities considered			
Recognised some need for planning	Worked in a very haphazard fashion			
Failed to discern need properly, or resources dimly recognised	Unsound choice, no recognition of resources etc.			
Shows some evidence of skill in limited area	Cannot recognise own limits or demands of project			
Significant areas omitted	Only a very shallow description			
Gives a very limited picture of the context of project	Gives little or no justification			
Little more than a diary	Shoddy and ill-organised			
Leaves something to be desired all round	Little recognition of role of illustration			
Only limited ability to review own progress	Unable to see actions in any other light			
Only limited ability to review own design	Unable to criticise own design			
Shows only limited ability	Unfortunately no real innate design ability			
Lower 25%	Bottom 10%			

Example 2

A personal view of the development of the Front Door project.*

Ken Baynes

Basic principles

I have never thought of the project as being concerned with a fixed quantum of architectural knowledge. I do not believe that a 'dose' of architectural facts and techniques will be effective in general education: to view the problem in this light is simply to repeat the mistake made by the majority of 'academic' subjects. We – thankfully – do not have to identify a series of examinable facts which the children must remember in order to be counted a success. Instead, we can concentrate on fostering direct experience, observation and active learning. The question is, experience what? observe what? learn how?

To my mind there are only two absolutely fundamental areas of experience where Front Door must help children to expand their concepts, confidence and experience. These are:

1 We need to foster an awareness of the environment as a three-dimensional reality. This kind of awareness is based on emotional, sensuous and intellectual experiences which, to be vivid, need to be felt at first hand. The major source of educational material can be Pimlico itself, though comparisons with other places and other cultures may also be useful. The key is direct street-corner observations and involvement, not looking at picture books.

* This is an extended version of a paper prepared for the Royal College of Art Summer School, 1975.

2 We need to present a picture of places being created not by chance but by human activity and human thought and decision. It is this aspect that should build up confidence in handling design concepts and relate the personal experiences of the first area to the more social, economic and technical aspects of planning and architecture. It is also the area that is the introduction to adult roles and responsibilities in the community.

I believe that both these areas are best approached through a project-based programme, which will be reminiscent of primary school work or, alternatively, of the kind of work done in art and design schools. In the secondary field, the Mode 3 CSE provides a model which encourages child-centred exploratory work. Here we attempt to bridge the gap. In these circumstances, it is easy to define the roles of the teacher and his architect colleague. These are:

1 To structure the opening stages of the project so that the children find themselves in a situation that catches their interest, leaves them free to behave creatively and provides them with a goal which will sustain their activities over an adequate period of time.

2 To work with the children during their enquiry providing, where necessary, specialist knowledge and skills.

3 To assist in the analysis, evaluation and presentation of the results of the children's work, working with the children.

It would be helpful if classes were allowed to break up naturally into groups or individuals for detailed work, but class-identity should be maintained and all work, individual or group, should, in the end, be a contribution to an overall co-operative effort.

The children's work should be valued and preserved as a contribution to expanding Pimlico's knowledge of itself and the possibilities for its future.

It is interesting to attempt to translate these general principles into programmes for the first, second and third years, each based on a single 12 or 13 week term, with three mixed-ability classes participating for the major part of a school afternoon.

First year

The first year project is to produce a giant class scrapbook on the reality of Pimlico. Each book could contain:

drawings

plans

rubbings

essays

the results of historical research

poems

political statements

surveys

questionnaires

photographs

pop-ups

ecological observations

traffic census

maps showing land use

recorded interviews

geographical analysis

minute observations of craft materials

studies of light, texture, colour

analysis of wildlife

comments on visits

observations on style

studies of historical buildings

studies of life in flats

studies of how people lived in the past in Pimlico

collections of ephemera

and many others the children would devise.

The three books would be exhibited at the end of each term, recorded on slides and lodged in the library for reference.

Programme (12 weeks)

1 Introduction. Group meeting of all three classes. Slide show. Teachers and architects introduced. Group discussion 'how to do it'. Brief for homework: 'What can we include in our scrapbooks?'

2 Class basis. Homework is the starting point. Practical discussion. How big can the book be? What materials can we use? Where can we go? What can we do? What's in the library/museums/streets? How can we use them? Class planning session. Brief for homework: 'What am I doing to contribute to our scrapbook?'

3 Class basis. Agree on individual and group work programmes. How to carry on in wet weather (resources, drawing in art rooms, slides, books, tapes etc). Work gradually begins.

4, 5 and 6 Work continues.

7 Class basis. How are we doing? Let's look again at what each of us has done. Are we doing enough? What more do we need to know? How are we going to find out? Does anyone

need to change what they are doing? Let's start to plan how the scrapbook will look.

8 and 9 Work continues. (an extra session if 13 weeks)

10 Finish it off, it's got to be ready to go in the book next week! Editorial problems discussed: does what we've done need an introduction/captions/ explanations? Who will write them – what should they say? Brief for homework: 'Come in next week with your contributions finished'.

11 All contributions exhibited on classroom walls. Each class views the work of all classes. Group discussion in each class of all the contributions. The contributions are brought together in a finally agreed sequence.

Teacher's homework: bind the book ready for next week.

12 Group meeting of all three classes. Triumphal entry of three scrapbooks. Brief talk. Show of films on London, American cities, how people live, how artists have shown cities. Some funny as well as serious films: Laurel and Hardy wrestling with the city environment and so on.

Second year

The second year project is to create an entertainment to tell the story of how and why Pimlico was built. This is envisaged as taking the form of a series of 'acts', perhaps each form would be responsible for three, probably arranged in chronological order, and obviously taking their inspiration from such social/historical 'musicals' as *Shut the Coalhouse Door* and *The Stirrings in Sheffield on Saturday Night*. However, as the work is under the auspices of the art

department, I imagine the light/sound tape/slide, back projection, masks, costume and drawings aspect would be particularly important. Perhaps there could be co-operation with the music department and outside theatre groups.

The result would be presented each term by the relevant three-form group to a school audience. A selection of the best acts from each group would be re-presented to a wider local audience at the end of the summer term.

Third year

The third year programme would be based on the idea of studying various human activities which affect and have to be accommodated in the environment. The aim would be to reveal the way in which the world of shops, houses and streets is adapted to human needs and to make some proposals about the way in which that adaptation could be improved. At this stage it would become appropriate to encourage individual rather than group study. Results might take the form of a study book, a collection of drawings, models of design proposals, tape/slide programmes, a folio of photographs, a series of paintings, recorded interviews, illustrated essays and so on.

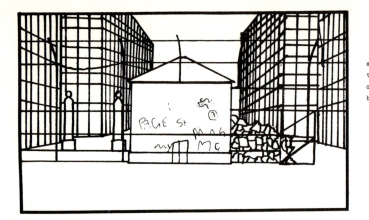

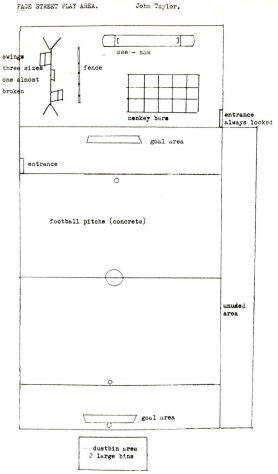

swings
three sizes
one almost
broken

fence

see - saw

monkey bars

entrance
always locked

goal area

entrance

football pitch (concrete)

unused
area

goal area

dustbin area
2 large bins

A part of the Front Door project at Pimlico School is an aspect of the Community Studies programme for fourth year pupils. A series of investigations is being carried out into the provision of various services in the neighbourhood of the school and proposals will eventually be prepared for their improvement. The design work will involve other groups and it is intended that at least some of the proposals will be carried through to the stage of implementation.

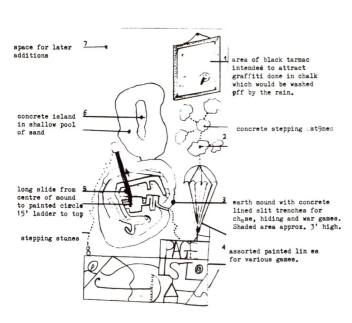

space for later   7
additions

area of black tarmac
intended to attract
graffiti done in chalk
which would be washed
off by the rain.

concrete island   6
in shallow pool
of sand

concrete stepping st9nes

long slide from   5
centre of mound
to painted circle
15' ladder to top

earth mound with concrete
lined slit trenches for
chase, hiding and war games.
Shaded area approx. 3' high.

stepping stones   8

assorted painted lin es
for various games.

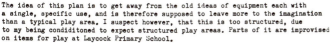

The idea of this plan is to get away from the old ideas of equipment each with
a single, specific use, and is therefore supposed to leave more to the imagination
than a typical play area. I suspect however, that this is too structured, due
to my being condiditoned to expect structured play areas. Parts of it are improvised
on items for play at Laycock Primary School.

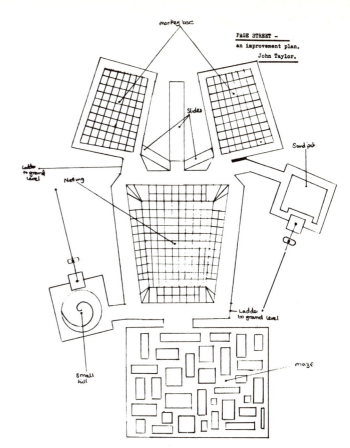

PAGE STREET -
an improvement plan.
John Taylor.

monkey bars

Slides

Sand pit

Ladder
to ground
level

Netting

Ladder
to ground level

maze

Small
hill

Shown here left and above are recorded
sheets made by fourth year pupils in the
first year of the scheme ; they are part of
a survey of play facilities.
(Inner London Education Authority)

Comment by a fourth year pupil :
Page Street play area is surrounded by
a high wire cage, which is broken in
many parts and very rusty, and could
cause some damage if you should happen
to stumble against the sharp broken bars
or put your hand in the wrong place. The
cage covers an area approximately
20 × 70 yards, covered by concrete, and
I have often seen it littered with broken
bottles and other rubbish. There is a
notice next to the dustbins which says it
is for children aged 7–11, but I do not
think it is a good place for children to
play.

Example 3

On the idea of problem solving*
Philip Roberts and John Harahan

Learning through activities that have been called 'designing', shares with the whole of the educational process the aim of promoting thought and personal growth by articulating possibilities for structuring experience.

If knowledge is in a state of continuous change how can we help children, and ourselves, develop attitudes, qualities, strengths, and insights appropriate to that condition?

An operational mechanism, for some, appears to lie in the development of 'problem solving' and we would like to focus on this, by asking a number of questions which we see as important and offering, in turn, some tentative answers for further discussion.

What constitutes a problem?
What constitutes a solution?

For discussion's sake, let us suppose that a typical activity might begin by the teacher asking the student or agreeing with the student's wish to 'make a chair' (or, try another object).

Is a chair a problem?
Or, is a chair a solution to a problem?
And if it is a solution, what then is the problem?
Or problems?
If it is a solution has the student considered other possible and valid responses?

And if 'yes', did he then redefine the problem? In other words, at what point did the student 'begin'?
Is a chair too particular, or can it throw light on the general?

Apart from techniques of questioning, are there other mechanisms, for example in synectics and in brain-storming, to help students to arrive at some distinction between 'problems' and 'solutions' and to appreciate their interaction?

If a chair is not a problem, how might we describe a problem?

Some would suggest that a problem is a description of the process of sensing gaps or disturbing missing elements. In this sense, a 'solution' is an acceptable degree of closure of the gap. The gap, or incompatibility, or problem space, might be variously described as the difference between performance required and performance available; between aspirations and available skills; between preferred conditions and a present situation.

Problem solving is understood by some to consist in a sequential step-by-step process.

For what kinds of problem might a step-by-step sequential 'design process' be sufficient?

Might the student be enabled to see a chair as a product within a system (the home)?
What is the relationship between product and system?
Does this suggest different kinds and levels of problem?
For instance, might it be helpful to consider the idea of the making of a chair as a technical-problem?
Is it still possible for one procedure to

be seen as appropriate to all problems?
Might a step-by-step procedure be most appropriate when there can be no possible deviation from a foreseen 'end'?
Is this kind of procedure algorithmic rather than heuristic?
Small scale and particular, rather than general?
Might there be differences in the structure of possible procedural approaches for, on the one hand, making *things* and on the other helping students expand their insights?
If there are differences, are they recognised by adults and by students?

Can students be enabled to move towards some recognition that a 'methodology' is useful, but only, sometimes sufficient?

Or is there a possibility that an attempt to provide a supportive structure for learning ('methodology') might be translated by an unacceptably large number of students and teachers as a closed prescription rather than as encouragement towards the opening of possibilities?

How can a 'method' (or '*the* method') be avoided and yet provide sufficient support for personal growth and change?

Or, might the question be one of enabling students to be at ease in a situation of risk? To enable them to undertake a practical consideration of the questions how? what? and why?

Can a situation which hopes to develop possibilities be evaluated?
What is to be evaluated; the experience, the product, or both?
And by whom?

* This is an extended version of a paper prepared for the Royal College of Art Summer School, 1975.

Children at work at Manor High
School where Phil Roberts teaches. In
the illustration on the left they are
evaluating a game that they have
designed.
(Photographs top left and right by
Peter Baistow)

Can problems be 'well defined'? Might that mean 'only sufficiently'?

For instance, does the student's learning consist in simultaneously structuring as well as 'solving' a problem, with the problem space being continually modified?

At what point, then, can a 'problem' be said to be solved or resolved, when 'its' context is a condition of change?

It might be suggested that 'a problem' is a part of a continuing process, upon which part our attention is presently focused.

Do the opportunities in problem solving offer to the student the sense of being in a dynamic process, in the short term consisting of interlocking problems and also in the long term with changing environmental and individual contexts?

If problem solving suggests a move away from the making of isolated products towards the consideration of products in their systemic context, what are the implications for the assumed parameters of subject boundaries?

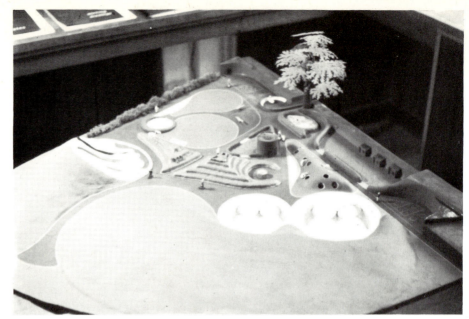

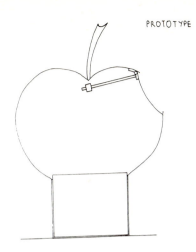

PROTOTYPE

STALK MADE FROM WOOD - DANGEROUS & WEAK.

BODY & BASE SEPARATE

BASE MADE FROM CARDBOARD COVERED IN PLASTIC.

PRODUCTION MODEL

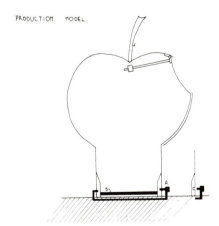

THE DOOR ON THE BASE (B) IS SCREWED IN

STALK MADE FROM RUBBER - SAFE

BODY & BASE - ONE PIECE MOULDING IN GLASS-FIBRE & ABS

DRAINAGE CHANNELS AT FRONT AND AT BASE OF STALK.

BIN FIXED DOWN BY BRACKET FIXED IN GROUND. WHEN A KEY

IS INSERTED AT 'A' THE BIN MAY BE LIFTED OUT.

Examples of project work carried out at Spondon School, Derbyshire, by two candidates for the Oxford A-level Design examination. John Harahan teaches at this school. In both cases, the pupils had to keep a careful record of each stage of the design development and to evaluate their achievement. These are excellent examples of the very high standard that can be expected in Fifth and Sixth form work.

Opposite page
Project 1 : design for a 'safety' playground to fit an actual site.

This page
Project 2 : designs and prototype for a waste bin for a children's playground. The 'apple' container is in 'Granny Smith' green with a white cover to the 'bite' or opening.

Although these three examples are very different in style and content, they appear to me to have a number of important characteristics in common. It is noteworthy that in no case is the discussion concerned with a closely defined end product. Even in the case of Front Door, which might appear more directed towards a particular outcome, the 'loose fit' of the programme's goals – 'an entertainment', for example – deliberately allows for the possibility of valuing a range of individual interests and motivations.

Design in these discussions is not being seen as a way of making any existing activity – craftwork or whatever – more relevant or palatable, but as an educational tool in itself. It is envisaged as being flexible enough to respond to the needs of any group of children and teachers. It is believed to be capable of engaging them in an exploration that will develop them and their capacities in a wide variety of ways. We can take as most significant the comment made by Malcolm Deere: 'what mature, rounded, *whole* people they are'. I do not think we should mistake this to mean that they are rounded and whole simply because they have had a deep experience of a body of knowledge that is normally neglected in general education. This is no doubt important, but even more to the point is this: 'it [the teaching relationship] is . . . based on the teacher learning *with* his students, on recognition of fallibility, on a kind of mutual respect.'

In notes written as a part of work on curriculum development, Philip Roberts* has attempted to spell out,

* From an unpublished thesis, 1975.

as carefully as possible, the really valuable aspects of the tripartite relationship between teacher, children and open-ended design activity. Here is what he had to say:

If we look at the work being done in school design departments, we might agree that much design work involves practical activity, and that learning is linked to doing. To some extent, the practical work is informed and accompanied by conscious mental activity: the line of distinction would be impossible to draw. We might hope, generally, that some preliminary thinking determines *whether* a pupil does practical work, and *what* the practical outcome might be. This affair between action and thought is the connexion between designing and active learning, and is essentially a dialectic . . .

The point about drawing attention to the process of designing, in education, is to help pupils make their learning situations more satisfying opportunities.

It is not to make the process more self-conscious, and mechanical. We want to go beyond that condition; absorb the process, and make it *less* self-conscious so that pupils can move autonomously. This is an important point to remember . . .

'So that pupils can move autonomously.' It is not just coincidence that this is an aim which, if translated into the adult world, could naturally stand for the democratic ideal in relation to design and technology. It is Ivan Illich who has expressed the connexion most clearly in his concept of 'conviviality'. Referring to the nature of this idea he said: 'I intend [it] to mean autonomous and creative intercourse amongst persons, and the intercourse of persons with their environment; and this in contrast with the conditioned response of

persons to the demands made upon them by others and by a man-made environment.' Here we reach the crux of the matter. It is clearly illogical to expect children to develop autonomy and creativity as a result of education if their school experience is confined solely to acquiring predetermined knowledge and skills and is not at all to do with handling value, quality, and the creation of new knowledge and new skills. This is where design makes its special contribution and provides what we might well describe as an 'alternative path' through a curriculum that is otherwise overloaded with the quantitative and the predictable.

Chapter 5

Self-help

In 1967 I ran the first of a series of one-term courses for teachers at what was then Hornsey College of Art. The subject was 'design education'. After discussions with my colleagues, Peter Green and Tony Horrocks, we decided that we would risk putting our convictions to the test. When the group of thirty assorted teachers arrived we faced them with an empty room, the use of a set of relatively well equipped workshops and studios, a secretariat, the bare minimum outline of a lecture programme, an argumentative tutorial staff, and two questions to which none of us knew the proper answers: 'What is design education?' and 'How do you run a course in it?'

We had blocked out the whole of the first of the twelve weeks we had available in 'tutorial discussions'. After that the plan was to arrange the course – workshop time, mini-courses, tutorials, visits, lectures – to a mutually agreed programme. Naturally there were many limitations and formidable difficulties. The agreed programme had to fit in with the already fixed programmes of the other courses that were running at the same time. It might not be possible, at short notice, to provide the kind of visits or speakers that the course members wanted. And people were momentarily confused by this upsetting of the normal teaching relationship. In the event, however, my main memory is of the tremendous excitement and creative energy that was released from the group – and from us, the tutorial team. The teachers on that particular course contributed attitudes and ideas that have continued to influence design education ever since.

There is a significant point to be made about the success of the experiment. The tutors never pretended *not* to know the answer to an important question if they knew it, and they never pretended they *did* know the answer if they did not. In short, the tutors were absorbed into the team and became part of what was really a miniature research group or 'think tank'.

Very few of the participants, who were mainly art and handicraft teachers, had had any direct experience of design activity before joining the course. They quickly identified this as being one of the main areas for development. Together we devised a series of 'situations', modelled on the design work then just beginning in schools, that would lead to an insight into the nature of designing. We took it to be our job to provide the background to do with design while they could best interpret its role in education. A number of the approaches we experimented with were effective and have now been taken back into classrooms and workshops.

It was this course that convinced me that 'self-help' was not only possible but that it was the only effective way of getting a realistic experience of design activity. It also convinced me that, once they had the relevant experience, teachers were more than capable of seeing the educational implications and of setting in train the work of curriculum development.

Since that experiment there have been other attempts at devising schemes for 'self-help' courses. Most of these depend even more on individual initiative. The Open University courses in design are of this kind. Effective use of them calls for a good deal of determination on the part of the student, who must enter fully into the design experiences that are offered and be prepared to develop his own powers of self-evaluation. The main problem here is the lack of a group of colleagues to provide a forum for debate, a source of encouragement when things go badly and a reservoir of varied experience.

These drawings were made by teachers on a course at Middlesex Polytechnic. They record the work they did collecting and analysing data about the design of seating. Activity of this kind is an excellent example of 'learning by doing' at the level of in-service training.
(Peter Green/Middlesex Polytechnic)

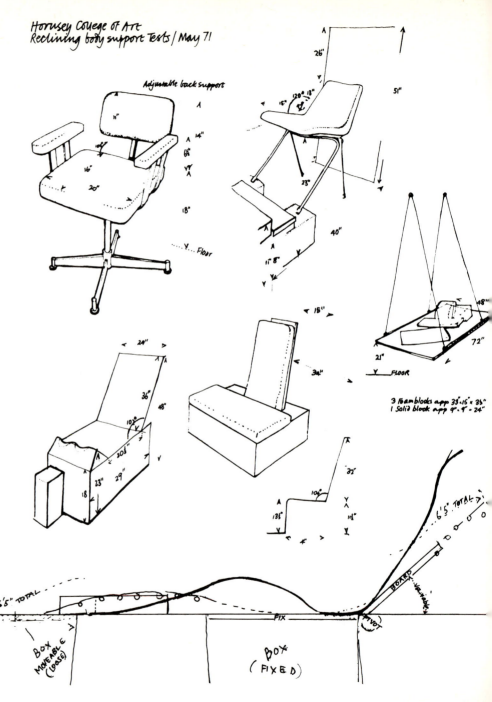

In 1971 I prepared a scheme for a self-help programme for design education that would operate on a national basis. In the event, this idea was replaced by the Design in General Education project at the Royal College of Art because, clearly, the greatest need at that point was for a careful evaluation of what had already been achieved. However, it is worth quoting the brief for the scheme here. It could still be effectively operated on a local level within a single education authority, or on a smaller scale by a

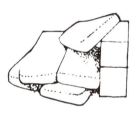

Foam blocks app. 33"·15"·3½"
Solid blocks each 8"·9"·24"

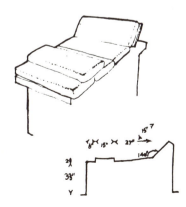

group of secondary schools working together:

Brief for Stage 1

In Stage 1 your group is asked to carry out a number of investigations, each of which is intended to help answer the question 'what is designing?' No suggestions are made as to method because the whole aim of the project is to test the possibility of self-education in design by practical activity. The discovery of appropriate methods by analysis and discussion is an important part of the process. It seems likely that some of this work will be done jointly with the pupils of the schools that are involved. Here the teacher may expect to work with his pupils or students as a team leader, and not in a didactic role. They will be exploring a situation together: neither teacher nor pupils can know the answers in advance.

Please keep a detailed record of each investigation: how it was organised; who did what; the methods that were used; the results obtained and what they revealed about the activity of designing. How to communicate the results is the final area for investigation in the project, and here, as before, a complete record should be kept.

Here are the proposed subjects for investigation:

1 Attitudes to design

Your group is asked to gather and evaluate people's opinions about designing and their attitudes to it. It is suggested that 'people' should include laymen from a very wide variety of social and economic backgrounds and also specialists – for example hospital administrators, architects, business executives, scientists and artists.

It may be found most practical to discover attitudes by asking people to review a number of particular designs, but good general surveys may also be possible.

2 Effects of design

Your group is asked to examine and evaluate a particular environment to see how it affects the people who use it. Where difficulties are seen to occur you are asked to suggest ways in which changes in organisation and design could bring about an improvement. If possible, put at least one of these changes into operation and assess whether or not it is successful. It is suggested that you select an environment with a quite complicated pattern of activities for this study, probably one where large numbers of people gather for short periods. Good examples would be a school dining hall, a hospital outpatients' department, the foyer and box office area of a cinema or theatre.

3 The activity of designing

Your group is asked, on the basis of small teams, to undertake a number of pieces of design work. It is essential that you should have a client. The client could be within the school (for example, the headmaster or mistress may need a new form of timetable presentation, waiting room furniture, a signposting system or even a complete new small building), or outside the school (for example, equipment for a nearby school for handicapped children, a 'zoo' for a primary school, or equipment for an old people's home). Make and evaluate a prototype, noting carefully

the comments of users. Please record the reasons for all the decisions you take whether or not these are reflected in the final designs, and also notice the *ways* (individual suggestion, client's suggestion, result of team discussion, copied from other designs) in which these decisions were reached. Please explain all your reasoning to the client at each stage and keep a record of his reactions and suggestions.

4 The results of the investigations

Your group is asked to analyse and then to communicate the results of your three investigations. Remember that the whole point is to reveal information about the nature of designing. The investigations should be looked at as a basis of experience from which to draw conclusions. It is suggested that a written report may not be the best or most entertaining method for communication: consideration could be given to film, slides with commentary, tape recordings, or a magazine-type presentation.

Please preserve *all* material produced during the investigations, even if it was discarded as useless at

Self-help education in design can often be turned to socially useful ends and involve collaboration between various parts of the educational system. The illustrations show a 'visual orientation game' designed by student teachers to help the children in an infants school, where there were many new immigrants, to get to know the locality of home and school.
(Peter Green/Middlesex Polytechnic)

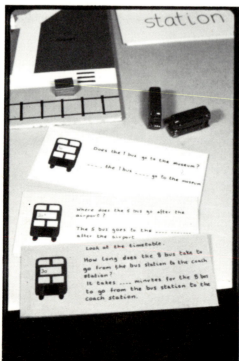

the time. It may well prove very interesting at the final discussion and evaluation stage.

Subsequent stages would have included curriculum development work based on the experience gained in Stage 1 and its extension into the formulation of examinations and new courses.

There is a good deal of evidence that this kind of activity can be successful. Groups exist in various parts of the country that have built up, completely from their own local resources, a substantial amount of experience in design and design education.

In this connexion, it is worth quoting again from Malcolm Deere's comments on his experience in acting as chief examiner for the Oxford A-level design paper. Speaking of curriculum development he had this to say:

The course is an interesting example of a public examination stimulating development from within: the usual course is almost the reverse of this. Bluntly, looking at Schools Council development projects, I find it hard to find many successes, and there have been very expensive failures. Our own experience has shown that doing the job can itself be more effective than setting up costly central teams. Rightly or wrongly I have seen my role as going beyond that of examiner: I have tried to operate as co-developer within a team of teachers, endeavouring to broadcast the results of experience and to codify findings. The most valuable form of progress can still be one or two teachers meeting informally together. The Oxford course can appear to be just another examination. In practice, I see it as a powerful, informal, example of curriculum development

within the field of design education. It proves nothing but it demonstrates a great deal of what is possible.

The response to the Royal College of Art's discussion papers provides further evidence of the potential of this 'self-help' approach. The papers were originally conceived of as being an efficient way of building up a realistic picture of what teachers in the field were thinking and doing. But after they had had a limited circulation as part of a pilot experiment it became clear that they, just like the Oxford course, contained considerable potential for curriculum development. Because the topics in the papers (see Table 4, pages 134 to 136) covered fundamental philosophical questions as well as detailed organisational ones, they helped to reveal the basic aims and attitudes of the people who discussed them. This revelation was often as important to these people themselves as to their colleagues. By the time the papers were due to be distributed widely, the decision had been taken to use them quite deliberately to promote curriculum discussions as well as to gather information. There was also the hope that they would be an effective means of bringing new teachers' groups into existence. Here is how this triple function was described in the papers:

The study team are aware of the fact that over the last few years a great deal of work on this theme [design education] has been done by schools, colleges, and local authorities. The situation exists where there is available a large reservoir of experience. It is the intention of those engaged in the study to make maximum use of this invaluable knowledge. It should be allowed to have a direct

influence on the formulation plans for the future.

This is more than a question of simply gathering together what already exists. Now that we have the chance to design the principles for development, there is a very strong argument for taking the opportunity to promote a nation-wide series of discussions among those who are already involved, and to base fresh plans on the outcome. In order to initiate the debate, the study team have prepared a set of discussion papers. In form they consist of a series of 'discussion areas' with associated questions. The topics range from aspects of the detailed organisation of integrated departments and attitudes in the classroom situation, to very broad social and philosophical points to do with the general validity of design as a part of general education . . .

The papers will have served a purpose if all they do is to encourage local groups – whether of teachers, administrators, advisers, lecturers, students or pupils – to look again at their educational aims and to relate them clearly to such crucial structural issues as facilities, staffing, examinations and curriculum development . . .

There are several forms which reports to the study team might take. The most basic is simply a letter which would give the views of an individual. But it is likely that some groups will want to make a more formal submission, perhaps consisting of factual reports and case histories from their own localities as well as general comments on the points raised in the discussion papers. Where this happens, the group may find that it needs to carry out enquiries of its own before reporting back to the RCA. This would widen the field of enquiry and would be welcomed by the study team.

Table 4

Selected areas from the discussion papers circulated to teachers and other educationists as a part of the 'Design in General Education' research project at the Royal College of Art

Discussion area 1

There exist specific conditions and attitudes in schools which may help or hinder the achievement of design awareness. It is important to make an accurate identification of what these are and to assess their importance. Only on such a basis can a practical plan for improvement be devised.

The following factors are suggested as significant. Please comment on their influence and, as far as possible, assess their relative importance:

1 The educational policy and character of the school as a whole and the relationship between this and individual areas of study

2 The curriculum of the school examinations and their interrelationship

3 The experience and attitude of the staff of the school: the staff/pupil ratio

4 The children at the school

5 The organisation of the school

6 The physical facilities of the school

7 The financial resources of the school as a whole and their availability to individual areas of study

8 Other resources of the school as a whole eg secretarial, library, and their availability to individual areas of study

9 The parents of the children at the school

10 The catchment area, the school and their interrelationship

11 The educational policy and character of the local authority

12 Awareness of local and national developments and resources

Discussion area 4

The traditional ethical and aesthetic values of art and craftsmanship have something to offer the contemporary world which it seriously lacks and increasingly wants. If departmental integration or other reorganisation under the banner of 'design' is involved, these areas must not suffer. Any resulting 'design department' must make it its duty to protect and foster the study of these as well as protecting and fostering the study of design. Such values, in general education, are complementary, not interchangeable.

Discussion points

1 Are art and craftsmanship likely to flourish best in 'departments' of their own or as part of a larger and, presumably, more powerful 'faculty' able to argue their case on the broadest possible basis?

2 What alternative groupings appear to offer attractive possibilities? Art as an element of a 'creative arts' faculty? Design with environmental studies and the workshops? Home economics and technical studies as an aspect of technology or applied science?

3 What are the implications of integration for specialist staff? Where are the 'heads or co-ordinators of faculty' to come from? What will be the roles and opportunities for the specialist in such a setting? What are the implications for teacher training?

Discussion area 6

In order to carry through the introduction of design studies, the schools require a large injection of design experience and confidence. In-service courses will be important here, but initial training should logically make a big contribution along with the opening up of teaching to people from industry and to people with qualifications in design and architecture. There is also the possibility of new links between practising architects and the schools.

Discussion points

1 Should there be specific courses for training teachers in 'design' or should the present pattern continue with its fundamentally 'art', 'handicraft' and 'home economics' emphases? Could an adequate coverage of design be integrated with this structure?

2 What pattern of in-service courses would be best adapted to teachers' needs? One-year courses? One-term courses? What topics should be included?

3 How could practising designers best contribute? By coming into the schools as teachers/consultants? By attempting to give clearer and more open descriptions of the problems, criteria and techniques involved in their work? By concentrating on work in teacher training?

Discussion area 7

In the end, the justification for promoting a widespread general design education intended to lead to the goal of 'design awareness' depends on a single proposition. It is that there exists an area of human experience, knowledge and action, centred on man's ability to use tools to mould the physical environment, which is as important to his existence as such well-recognised areas of learning as numeracy and literacy.

Discussion points

1 What evidence can be found to support this proposition? Can relevant examples be drawn from a study of historical and contemporary society?

2 In his book *Art and Society*, Herbert Read speaks of art as being a 'mode of knowledge' distinct from mathematics, science or literature. Does the use of tools to mould the environment and create a human habitat indicate a similarly well-defined area? How far does it overlap such traditional categories as art, architecture, movement and dress, husbandry and craftsmanship?

3 Does ability in this area depend on the specific development of skills and attitudes identifiable in the make-up of human beings? In short, is it possible to educate for a better performance and higher level of awareness in this sphere?

4 Is it possible to make a clear statement about what characteristics might be displayed by 'an educated man or woman' in this area of knowledge?

Discussion area 8

It is important to recognise that, apart from its status as a 'mode of knowledge' and its importance in relation to contemporary problems, design awareness also offers important experiences for the personal development and general education of the individual. There is the sensuous, physical and perceptual aspect of the world of materials, craftsmanship and spatial dimensions. There is also the analytical methodology of design which offers a practical insight into mathematics, logic, orderly planning and communication. And there is design's ability to focus on the environmental aspect of man's social, moral, aesthetic and economic actions.

Discussion points

1 What are the elements of design awareness which could contribute most to the general intellectual and emotional development of the individual?

2 How can these general advantages of design awareness best be made better known? What contribution could they make to the modern school curriculum?

3 Schools habitually use elements of design as an integral part of other subjects – graphics, for example, in maps, diagrams and notebooks in most areas of study. What might be done to make such a range more coherent and better related to the broader topic of design awareness and visual communication?

The papers served their purpose and the results were impressive. They reinforced the conviction that, given an appropriate impetus, teachers were quite capable of using their local resources to carry out effective curriculum development and devising useful tools for self-help in the process. In some cases, groups of teachers spent a dozen evening sessions on the points raised while others submitted their views at book length. Still others sent sound or video tapes of their discussions. As a result, the material available to the research team provided an extraordinarily vivid profile of the hopes, fears, aspirations and attitudes of teachers in art, craft and design and home economics. But what it did most of all was to provide concrete evidence that here was a body of people who had amongst them relevant skills and experiences that could be enlarged relatively easily to embrace a flexible and effective knowledge of design education and design activity.

Here we need to introduce a further element into the concept of 'self-help'. It is to do with the 'body of knowledge' that can be said to constitute design. We have already looked at the claim that the primary body of knowledge consists of the actual buildings men have erected and the products they have made. If the point is accepted, it means that every one of us is, in fact, living in a vast textbook covering the history and development of design. Local groups should be encouraged to look first at their own surroundings, to understand the attitudes and decisions that created them, and then to be involved in their future existence and adaptation. The logic of design awareness appears to indicate that it

is best to start from those vivid elements in one's own experience that constitute direct technical and aesthetic experience and to build outwards from these rather than vice versa. Architectural guides to Florence or Blenheim Palace are only second best; the real stuff of design is to be found on every front porch, in every backyard, in the local factory and the municipal park.

In the present financial climate there seems no doubt that a great deal of knowledge and confidence about design will have to be gained by teachers while still on the job. More short courses would help, as would greater, and more systematic, emphasis on design studies in colleges of education and colleges of art and design. But most teachers will have to rely on reading and on working with their own pupils and colleagues. Fortunately, design is well adapted to this kind of approach.

No doubt a good deal will be done to help teachers in this position, but in the long term, a continuing link will have to be sought between the work of designers and the work of educationalists. It is even possible to foresee a time when the two areas will become almost synonymous. Designers are increasingly dissatisfied with the esotericism of their activities and are looking for ways to involve users and the general public in the decisions that they are making. Educationalists are seeking greater realism, and greater relevance to life. There is here an obvious area for joint exploration and research; one that could lead to a genuine democratisation of the design process and a related release of energy into practical education.

There is a widespread interest in socially useful design projects amongst student teachers as well as student designers. Shown here and opposite are two examples from the Department of Creative Design at Loughborough College of Education.

A structure designed by a student on the teachers' certificate course. It is to provide a light and easily erected shelter for use in the event of natural or man-made disasters. The structure inflates by means of a vacuum cleaner, car exhaust or foot pump and can be covered with light plastic sheeting.

*A constructional toy designed by a
student on the teachers' degree course.
It is based on a 'Meccano' principle and
is intended for use in a youth club. Full
size objects can be made and
motorised by a lawn mower engine.*

It is for this reason that the Royal College of Art report has endorsed so strongly the concept of local groups as the basis for effective curriculum development. The proposal is for a series of centres of research and development in secondary education throughout the country. These would involve designers and industrialists as well as teachers and other educationalists. By the time this book appears several of these regional centres should have come into being. Each of them would have a triple function:

1 They would act as agents to promote and support design education in their own areas

2 They would contribute to a major, centrally managed, research project into the relationship between design activity and learning and into the relationship between child development and the experiences and performances involved in practical, aesthetic, environmental and technical education

3 They would each be responsible for one specific area of research and development (for example, architectural education) which they would organise and carry out, making the results directly available to the other centres and also nationally

For the individual teacher, the significance of such a regional network would be its ability to sponsor meetings and activities and to draw teachers and designers together. It would, however, be ineffective unless it also led to activity at the level of groups of schools working together; at the level of teachers in a single school working together; and at the level of a teacher and pupils working together in the setting and opportunities of their own particular classroom or workshop.

As we have already seen in the previous chapter it is in the nature of design activity to change the relationship between the teacher and the taught and to make them partners in a learning exploratory enterprise.

Phil Roberts puts it this way:

Pupils (and teachers) will be in situations through which they will experience (open-ended, evaluative) situations analysing their constraints and defining their values for an acceptable change . . .

In other words, they will be active learners through an approach which unites the experience of designing and learning. Of necessity they will experience the instability, the diversity, the confrontation, the validity of possible response, rather than 'right' answers, and that both designing and learning (if any distinction can be made) are essentially to do with change.

The correspondence between designing and learning offers radical possibilities, and provides the focus for change in this area of the secondary curriculum.

Here is a glimpse of a situation in which the classroom becomes a place where children *and* teachers learn together and where change and the free development of the curriculum become normal, everyday experiences. This is surely as it should be. It is hard to accept that curriculum changes should appear as unexpected upheavals to be approached with fear and trepidation. What is basically lacking at the moment is a set of techniques and concepts for handling change with confidence. It is just this experience that design activity is capable of providing. It is in this sense that design activity and group working provide a natural 'workshop' for curriculum development, for self-education and self-help.

Chapter 6

The future of design

If design is interpreted in the broad sense used in this book, then it is strikingly obvious that many of the problems and crises facing the modern world are sharply reflected in it. Design is to do with the right use of resources. Design is about the application of technology to resources so that they can be converted into a physical world that extends mankind's aspirations and 'humanises' nature. Design is to do with the resolution of conflicts between people who have varying degrees of access to resources and technology. In short, design is to do with one aspect of the two fundamental questions which are posed to the members of every civilisation: 'What do you value?, How do you want to live?' To which we, living in our scientific and technological age, can add a question that is more specifically for us: 'How do you propose to use your expanded knowledge and extended power to improve the content of life on earth? How can you place the quantitative more decisively at the service of the qualitative?'

The direct elements in the crisis facing the world are easy to identify. It is also easy to recognise the ones that affect the future of design. They have been well known for at least a decade. They are as follows:

1 The natural resources of planet earth are limited

2 The population of the planet is growing at a dramatic rate: there seems to be no prospect that resources can do the same

3 Even if science and technology *could* stretch resources sufficiently, the resulting pollution would be likely to destroy civilised life

To this picture of crude shortage we can add other elements that further define the character of the environmental crisis and that limit the possible courses of action which are open to us:

1 The world is economically divided into the 'haves' and the 'have nots'. The division is cruel, arbitrary and extreme. There is no likelihood that a peaceful solution to environmental problems can be found unless the solution *also* contributes to a redress of this intolerable injustice

2 The world economy appears to be founded on growth. But unlimited growth is, in the long term, impossible. At the moment, however, any reduction in growth in the rich countries causes only relative discomfort there, while in the poor countries it causes disaster, starvation and death

3 The importance of growth has led to the creation of cultural forms (notably advertising) that promote trivial consumption and heedless greed. In so far as such attitudes are institutionalised and go deep in the rich countries, they present an

"Lord how this world improves as we grow older"

Although the resources of the planet are limited and are used in a way which is grossly unfair, they continue to be expended at an alarming rate by the industrial world's dependence on, and fascination with, high technology. Can a transformed technology be used to solve this problem which technology has itself created? There probably is no other alternative.

Above
The fascination and related alarm are not new. 'Lord how this world improves as we grow older.' A cartoon from the early days of the Industrial Revolution. (The Museum of London)

Opposite right
Walking in the Heavens. From the Toronto 'Telegram', 8 June, 1965. (John Frost Collection)

Opposite far right
Rubbish. (Chris Ridley)

intractable spiritual problem that future generations will find it difficult to solve.

But there is more to it than this. Design is not simply instrumental. It is not only a tool directed at the world's environmental problems. It is also, when put in a full context of workmanship and direct creative activity, a way of entering into life; a way of experiencing an indispensable part of life's meaning and content. It is not only a way of doing, it is also a way of knowing and a way of being. This means that its evocation in the life of any individual – and so of society – has to depend on deeply internalising experiences to do with aesthetics, tools and materials, decision-making, conceptualising and qualitative evaluation. If these are not internalised nothing substantial can happen.

An important aspect of the present crisis is that more and more design activity is being wrenched apart from these deep roots in experience. Design, like work, is becoming alienated from a direct experience of tools, materials and creative involvement in their use. An element in the equation 'boring work = extended leisure' has been to reduce craft to the level of decoration and so to remove its vital insights about resources, aesthetics and tools from the central arena of economic life and, as a result, from the formative experience of the designer.

We have already seen, in Chapter 3, how deeply developments connected with the division of labour have affected the work experience of most people living in industrialised society. And we have seen how the same developments have militated against democratic involvement. They have resulted in a real concentration of power in the hands of a few specialists. Here again, the deprivation of experience and involvement means that many people have missed just those formative experiences that would be valuable in the future in resolving the design aspects of the environmental crisis.

Technological fantasy. Covers of science fiction magazines. (Eduardo Paolozzi)

How do we see the future? How do we want to live? How can we use technology to improve the quality of life? It is unfortunate that the majority of fictional visions of the future are pessimistic. They appear to envisage an inexorable progress of technology accompanied by a related reduction in individuality and personal freedom. At times this is a vision that, in the twentieth century, has come perilously close to reality.

Above
A still from Fritz Lang's film
'Metropolis'.
(Transit Filmgesellschaft MBH)

Over page
Nazi march past from Leni Reifenstahl's
'Triumph of the Will'.
(National Film Archive)

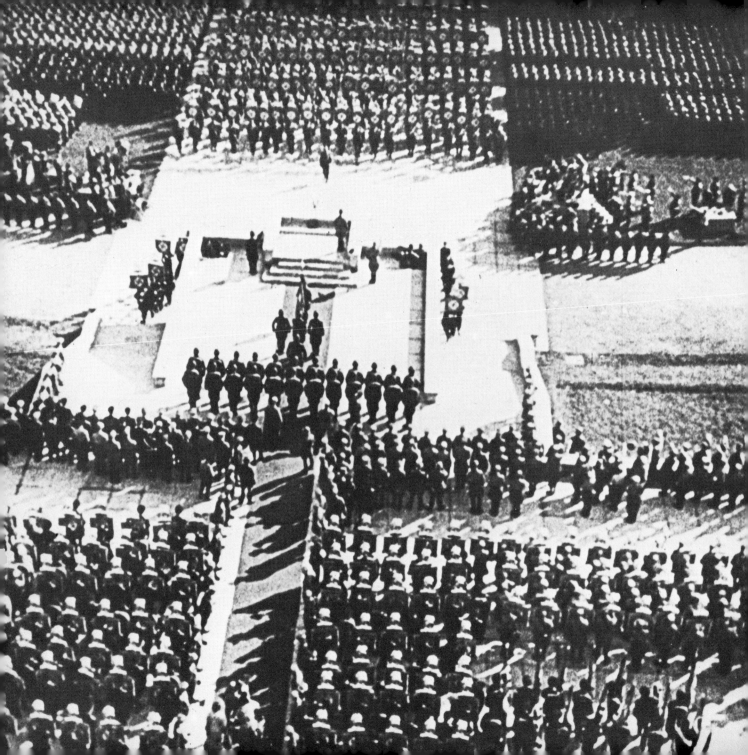

It is, of course, naive as well as fatalistic and despairing to imagine that the tendencies that I have just described are inexorable. It is not inevitable that an existing trend will continue into the future. The whole history of design and technology shows that such trends frequently end, or are reversed, in ways that are unpredictable. Market forces control shortages by the brutal effects of inflation. But the impending crisis means that we need to attempt to direct the changes in ways that do not simply save us from disaster but that also take us along routes that reflect our highest aspirations and ideals.

In the immediate past the world has always looked to technology to help it to force its way out of any environmental or economic impasse. Now the conviction is growing that the bill for being so spendthrift in the past will have to be paid. In any case, we can see that the present impasse is one which technology has itself helped to create. It is not hard to imagine that we are now at a moment in history as decisive for us as the Industrial Revolution was for our ancestors nearly two hundred years ago. Technology transformed life then; perhaps life may now be about to transform technology. We may guess that technology and industry will continue to play a vital role but that this role will be very different from that which exists today.

If something of this kind is true, then the impact on the character of design and design education will be revolutionary. It is already quite clear that there will be changes affecting the content of design activity, the role of the design professions and the whole of the world-wide political and educational structure wherever it supports decision-making processes that are relevant to the environment.

These changes are beginning. Taken together they constitute what might be called a 'change of consciousness' about our relationship with the environment and our dependence on technologies that contain no element of conservation. The people who have made a dramatic contribution to this are now well known – Rachel Carson, Buckminster Fuller, Victor Papanek, Ivan Illich, to name what is an inevitably arbitrary selection. What they have been saying, at first with few listeners, has now become the common property of millions in the industrialised countries who have benefited from the great power of the mass media to disseminate and popularise. But it is also significant that they have been willing to listen. What they have heard has clearly coincided with their own deep feelings and their direct experience of life in a predominantly wasteful and materialistic economy.

Man and Building. This is a contemporary reality. (Chris Ridley)

Whether or not we can create civilised conditions in the future will depend on our own consciousness of how life might be lived and what our relationship might be with the natural world from which we have developed. In this, education is vital because the potentialities are not always visible in the places where the majority of people grow up. It is the ability to make an imaginative leap into an unknown but more balanced future that design education has to succeed in fostering.

Right
Where we grow up affects us for better or worse. It limits our experience and moulds our ability to think creatively about 'what might be'. It is up to education to expand on what is available without abandoning what are often strong cultural roots. (Chris Ridley)

Left
In a civilisation full of waste, everything can easily be seen as junk. (Chris Ridley)

The exciting thing is that their response has not been to withdraw into uncomprehending anger. Their response has been creative. In 1959, when still a student, I took a small part in one of the first effective popular fights to have a planning application rejected on aesthetic and environmental grounds: a mixed group of objectors had the design for a disastrous building for Piccadilly Circus thrown out at a public enquiry. Since then such successes have become commonplace and have contributed enormously to the quality of town and country. Even if individual battles have often been lost, and even if efforts have sometimes been misdirected, the significant point is that a variety of appropriate institutions have been created and a vast amount of skill and knowledge has been accumulated for the future. This widespread struggle against public and private vandals, which has gone on constantly during the past fifteen years, will probably appear to succeeding generations to have been of vital importance. The movement for preservation and conservation has provided a particularly appropriate workshop for the development of *practical* techniques for affecting decisions about the man-made environment at local level.

The movement to preserve has not only been a matter of protest and objection. It has also provided a market for the maintenance of a number of rare craft skills and sometimes a basis for their wider dissemination to enthusiastic amateurs. This is a good thing in itself, but its real significance goes deeper. The people involved have had the opportunity to work to standards of finish and quality that transcend economic necessity. They have thus had, in reclaiming old canals, restoring ancient buildings and rebuilding outmoded machinery, a deeply civilising experience. At the same time, they have contributed to the variety, drama and beauty of the environment. Here again, we can recognise the emergence of a kind of behaviour that provides a storehouse of valuable precedents and the possibility of considerable expansion beyond the confines of preservation.

There has also been a growing fascination with the idea of an 'alternative' society. Sometimes this has been nothing more than a romantic nostalgia for a lost rural innocence that never truly existed in the past. The desire to return to 'self-sufficiency', when interpreted as a return to subsistence agriculture, is not a very helpful or creative concept. It is an approach that would condemn the already poor areas of the world to total collapse. Where these alternative visions provide immeasurably valuable ideas is to be found in their ability to distinguish between varying possible degrees of technological intervention and sophistication and in their attempt to spell out the implications of each 'mix' of such technologies for the future quality of life on earth.

It appears to be a characteristic of these alternative visions that they look to men and women, the sun, the wind and the movement of water as the appropriate sources of power. All seek a new and more mutually creative relationship between man, the tools he uses and the earth that he inhabits. We can compare the sails,

Opposite above
Affection : nineteenth century brooch.

Opposite below
Rape : a modern landscape.

Above
Care : another modern landscape, the garden of a home for old people in South London.
(Chris Ridley)

Alternative visions of man and nature. How we see the relationship will determine what the future of design will be concerned with.

barrages and bicycle technology of this picture of the future with our existing technology of extraction and massive energy consumption. What is immediately clear is that in choosing a particular technological mix we are also choosing a set of values and adopting a group of beliefs about our relationships with other people. The significant moral element in the alternative visions of a future society is that they imply the development of technologies that can be shared between rich and poor countries. They imply less, not more, specialisation. And they mean a lessening of raw consumption in the industrialised countries.

At the moment we still lack a convincing picture of how the world might be led, political step by political step, away from a centralised high technology concentrating riches in industrial countries but using up the resources of the whole world. The goal, if we could get there, would be a decentralised 'medium' technology that would spread the wealth and power it created while conserving resources. But what the supporters of alternative societies have done is to show convincingly enough that, given the will, the time and the manpower, an appropriate technology could be brought into existence and that it might be capable of producing enough power to support a full and civilised style of life.

It is hardly surprising that the environmental crisis is causing the deepest possible heart-searching amongst professional designers of every kind. A frank acknowledgement of mistakes made during the immediate past and a feeling of frustration that so much talent and opportunity have been wasted have emerged. Designers are sensitive to the fact that they have undertaken roles that have encouraged waste rather than reduced it. They are conscious of being identified as one of 'them' and not as one of 'us'. Above all, there is the traumatic realisation that the skills of planning and design that have been expended on building since 1945 have failed to create an urban environment that people can enjoy or even, in some cases, tolerate. This is a massive failure and it will take years before the real meaning of it can be properly digested and evaluated.

Designers have been amongst those who have played a leading part in bringing about the 'change of consciousness' we have been discussing. Their arguments have been directed at their clients as well as at the general public. What is happening now is that a degree of independent action is being sought in the initiation of design projects. There are small institutional beginnings that could quickly grow. Such a development would be full of hope for the future, but the major conceptual breakthrough is to be found in the awareness that there is a major area of development for design that may have to be pursued, at least at first, independently of narrowly defined commercial pressures and requirements.

The recognition that this is so is put clearly in, for example, the thematic statement for the international symposium on *Design for Need* which was held in London in 1976. Here is what it said:

The symposium will provide an opportunity to demonstrate and explore the contribution which design can make to the needs of mankind.

There is the world-wide concern that, despite the material benefits arising from advanced technology and industry, there is a deterioration in the quality of life and failure in the provision of many essential needs. This is accompanied by an increasing awareness of a waste of resources and a despoilation of the environment. Among the reasons for examining the contribution of design in this situation are:

Design is the essential creative and formative element in the technological complex, and, as such, must be regarded as a major contributor to the performance of industry in the service of mankind.

Design is usually seen as a secondary activity responding to the requirements of governmental and industrial organisations who are largely responsible for the initiation of design and the formulation of briefs. More recently, however, there have been examples of the design schools and of professional designers initiating design projects and developments in response to an awareness of social needs not otherwise being fulfilled. This is a return to the earlier ideals of the profession of industrial design which aimed to meet the needs of the modern world by designing in human terms where social purpose combined with aesthetic expression and symbolic value.

Table 5, opposite, also taken from the programme, lists some of the areas where the organisers of *Design for Need* believe that pressing problems are likely to be found. It is clear that they are a mixed bag. Some are to do with correcting the errors of past design and social policy, others are to do with developing the technology and the products that might be required for the creation of a new social policy.

Some are to do with 'systems' problems involving complex issues of appreciation – problems that are never finally 'solved'. Others are to do with specific areas of technological innovation, such as devices to tap new energy sources. It is easy to see that there is an interrelationship between these various categories. The realisation of any kind of alternative society in the future will depend on the hard-headed practicality of the detailed design work that goes into its supporting technology. It is this detail that will determine the pattern and content of the 'systems' that emerge. At the same time, a degree of success in the amelioration and improvement of existing systems will give experience and confidence for the future. Properly directed, such success could also lead to the translation into practical politics of the first steps away from the environmental crisis.

Table 5

DESIGN FOR NEED

The main subjects are listed below with some examples of possible projects within each area. These examples are not intended to be restrictive and it is hoped that the symposium and exhibition will provide the opportunity for enlargement of the total field.

Urban Environment

Studies in the improvement of the urban environment

New developments, conservation and subtractive design: streets, traffic, shopping, parks, leisure

Natural Environment

Studies in the improvement and conservation of the natural environment

Identification of regional characteristics

Problems of tourism and recreation

Wild life

The effects of agricultural industries and the growth of populations

Community Problems

The human problems arising from living in cities in remote or small communities

Access to facilities

Alienation and vandalism

Isolation of the elderly

Provision of adventure and physical release for the young

Transport

Public and personal transport

Environmental and social effects of mass transport

Noise and pollution

Development of alternative systems

Pollution, Waste and Recycling

Devices for the detection and measurement of pollution

Reduction of pollution: collection, utilisation and disposal of waste

Design of recyclable products and systems

Resources and Energy

Studies in the economic uses of energy and resources

Development of alternative forms of energy

Medical Equipment

Studies in diagnostic, nursing and clinical equipment for domestic, hospital and emergency use

Aid for the Handicapped

Studies in prosthetic aids and other systems for use in the home, travelling, at work and in education and leisure

Safety

Studies in safety aids and other systems for use in the home, travelling, at work and in education and leisure

Disaster Relief

Equipment, systems and communication aids for use in major accidents and natural disasters

Regional Development Areas

Studies in the use of design to stimulate or regenerate local industries and employment

Developing Countries

Studies in equipment and systems for use in housing, agriculture, industry, transport, education, in developing countries

Education

Studies in educational equipment and systems

Aids to literacy

Language tuition for immigrant communities

In this context, it is worth reminding ourselves, finally, of some of the points made in Chapter 4 and the concluding sections of Chapter 3. There we saw how liberal assumptions in design are already running parallel with those in education. It is when we look to the future that the real significance of this becomes clear. It is then that the crucial advantages of an aesthetic, practical, workshop or studio-based education really come into focus. Phil Roberts speaks of 'design education at the level of the whole community leading to the participation by one and all in environmental decisions'. What this implies is a fundamental shift of power and a vast 'opening out' of the experience of design, making and doing.

This opening out could not but have a dramatic effect on our relationships with one another and our environment. It could provide us with the means to transcend the present crisis and, perhaps, even to use it to our long-term advantage.

There have been various suggestions in the last few years for the establishment of 'architectural appreciation centres' or similar institutions. If this means little more than a building to house didactic exhibitions about the history of building, modern planning and contemporary ecological problems it will be a useful but not a decisive development. A more effective vision would be the creation of a new kind of 'design centre'. This would not be a place where people went only to see displays of what they might buy. It would be a place principally to engage directly in designing and making. In the centre people would be able to

obtain free advice on ecology, planning, do-it-yourself and resistance to official vandalism. They would be able to practise any craft from macramé to cooking, or from stained glass to gardening. There would be a technological workshop, an energy resources centre, a consumer advice bureau and, very important, a forum where the constituents of 'them' and 'us' could meet together on an equal footing to thrash out a new kind of creative approach to the environment.

The basis for such centres already exists in the nationwide network of secondary schools and the related institutions in further and higher education. Their evolution would be the natural extension of the local curriculum development groups described in Chapter 5. Throughout the country the necessary practical facilities exist. So, in embryo, do the relevant programmes in schools, technical colleges and evening institutes. The ideas involved in design activities and awareness would provide the catalyst for further growth. With only a little governmental support and encouragement this network could be expanded and made vastly more effective. The resulting excitement could create the energy once again to place architecture, planning, design and workmanship back where they belong at the centre of the community's concern for its own development.

In detail this conception of 'design centres' may not be right. There are other patterns that could work. The suggestion stands here for the connexions we need to make. It suggests that they could best be made

through the education system and on the basis of the pioneering work that has already been done on design education in schools. Enlarged and extended, this background provides the experiences we need.

Although each of the various aspects of the 'change in consciousness' appears to be hopeful, it is also plain that, as a basis for the future, they are incoherent and at an early stage of development. The potential is there, but many people will doubt if it can be brought to fruition. It is in precisely this connexion that the role of design education, which represents a 'change of consciousness' in schools, appears to be the necessary cohesive element.

Books for further reading

The list of books given below is short; there are only twenty in all. The number of books on design is now relatively large and growing every year. I have made no attempt to be exhaustive and I have not tried to deal with books on design education as such; good lists of these are available from the National Association for Design Education and the Design Council. Instead, I have included only those books on design that have had a dramatic effect on my own thinking, or those that I believe to be entertaining as well as useful. For me, they would form something of a minimum reading requirement – but not, I hope, an impossible one.

Man-made Futures: Readings in Society, Technology and Design. Edited by Nigel Cross, David Elliott and Robin Roy. Hutchinson Educational, The Open University Press, 1974

The series of **Design Bulletins** compiled by the Department of the Environment. HMSO (various titles since 1962)

The Making of the English Landscape W G Hoskins. Originally published 1955. Penguin, 1970

Garden Cities of Tomorrow Ebenezer Howard. A new paperback edition. Faber and Faber, 1966

The Death and Life of Great American Cities Jane Jacobs. Penguin, 1964

Design Methods: Seeds of Human Futures. J Christopher Jones. Wiley-Interscience, 1970

Art and the Industrial Revolution Francis Klingender. Originally published 1947. Revised edition by Sir Arthur Elton. Evelyn Adams and Mackay, 1968

The Gutenberg Galaxy Marshall McLuhan. Routledge & Kegan Paul, 1962

Understanding Media Marshall McLuhan. Routledge & Kegan Paul, 1966

News From Nowhere William Morris. A new paperback edition. Routledge & Kegan Paul, 1970

The City in History Lewis Mumford. Originally published 1961. Penguin, 1966

Design Methods Manual Man-made Futures course, Units 13–16. The Open University, 1975

Design Project Guide Man-made Futures Course, Unit 12. The Open University, 1975

Pioneers of Modern Design
Nikolaus Pevsner. Originally
published 1936. Penguin, 1960

**The Nature and Art of
Workmanship** David Pye.
Cambridge University Press, 1968

The Nature of Design David Pye.
Studio Vista, 1964

The Roots of Modern Design:
Functional Tradition in the
Nineteenth Century. Herwin
Schaefer. Studio Vista, 1970

The Wheelwrights Shop George
Sturt. Originally published 1923.
Cambridge University Press, 1963

The Long Revolution Raymond
Williams. Penguin, 1965

**Kandy-Kolored Tangerine Flake
Streamline Baby** Tom Wolfe. Cape,
1966

When looking at the future of
design, I would say that it is
particularly important to keep abreast
of work by Buckminster Fuller, Bruce
Archer, Christopher Jones, Simon
Nicholson, Ivan Illich, Victor
Papanek and E F Schumacher.

Other books on art and design by Ken
Baynes:

Art in Society
Art and Society 1: War
Art and Society 2: Work
Art and Society 3: Worship
Art and Society 4: Sex

Edited by Ken Baynes:

Attitudes in Design Education
**Hospital Research and Briefing
Problems**
**Evaluating New Hospital
Buildings**
Scoop, Scandal and Strife: an
analysis of photography in
newspapers

Acknowledgements

A lot of people have contributed to this book. I think first of all of the teachers I have worked with in the past eight years: it is they who have established design education in schools and made it a force in general education. In far from ideal circumstances, they have laid a firm foundation for the future. Next I think of my colleagues in the immediate past. For two and a half years, until April 1976, I was a research fellow at the Royal College of Art working with Professor Bruce Archer and Richard Langdon. This was an important experience for me – a hectic period of research and travel during which new concepts took shape and the philosophy of design education was gradually hammered out. I am pleased to have had their help and friendship and I am specially grateful to the Rector, Lord Esher, for his very generous foreword. I know we all hope that time will show we have made a useful contribution to the future education of children in Britain.

My first contact with design education was when I went with my wife, Kate, to Leicestershire. We had been commissioned by John Blake to write an article for *Design* magazine. There we met Bernard Aylward and his wife. At that time, Bernard was county design adviser and it was in his company that we visited the new 'design faculties' that Leicestershire was creating in its comprehensive schools. The visit set a pattern. Kate

has continued to be closely involved. Without her indispensable help and support, I could not have achieved anything. Bernard has been a continuing inspiration to me. He is practical and idealistic at one and the same time and has always been optimistic, believing that improvement, however small, is possible and worth-while. I believe that he has made one of the essential contributions to the development of design education and it has been a great pleasure to work with him. And, in a wide variety of ways, the Design Council has continued to give help and support, culminating in the present book.

The book itself has been a pleasure to work on. The editorial team at the Design Council has made possible an exceptionally smooth development from concept to reality. I am very grateful to them for their help. In my own studio, Pauline Riley has coped calmly with every emergency, sorted out my spelling, and has indomitably prepared the final manuscript from the inevitable maze of erasures and second thoughts that scored the original in a patina of multi-coloured inks.

About Design would be useless without its illustrations. I am grateful to all the many individuals and institutions who have allowed me to reproduce photographs and drawings. They are credited in the captions, but some special thanks are due. First, to my friend Chris Ridley. I have worked with him for many years and have always enjoyed the photographs that he has created. Here again, he has made a big contribution. Second, to one of my clients, King Edward's Hospital Fund for London. They have generously allowed me to reproduce a series of illustrations from a book on hospital development that I designed for them. Finally to the many teachers who have contributed material. Their help has been especially valuable, and I appreciate it particularly because I well understand the time it has taken to prepare under the pressures of school life.

I have included a number of quotations in the book. I am grateful to the following for permission to quote: American Heritage Publishing Co Inc for an extract from 'The Penguin Book of the Middle Ages' by Morris Bishop © 1968, American Heritage Publishing Co Inc; Bruce Archer; Associated Business Programmes Ltd for an extract from 'The Management of Conflict' reprinted in 'Making Institutions Work' by Sir Geoffrey Vickers (London 1973); Malcolm Deere; J M Dent & Sons Ltd and Little Brown & Co for 'The People Upstairs' by Ogden Nash from 'Versus'; Elsevier Scientific Publishing Company, Amsterdam, for an extract from 'Dilemmas in a General Theory of Planning' by Horst Rittel and Melvin Webber from 'Policy Sciences 4' (1973) pp. 155–169; Peter Green for an extract from an article published in 'Design Education'; John Harahan; G B Harrison; Hodder & Stoughton Ltd for an extract from 'The Making of the English Landscape' by W G Hoskins; John McHale for an extract from 'World Facts and Trends' published in 'Futures'; Lund Humphries Publishers Ltd and Overlook Press for an extract from 'Art and Society' by Ken Baynes; Penguin Books Ltd for an extract from Plato's 'Republic' translated by H D P Lee © H D P Lee 1955; Sir Nikolaus Pevsner for an extract from 'Pioneers of Modern Design' published by Penguin Books Ltd; Don Porter; Praeger Publishers Inc for an extract from 'The Roots of Modern Design' by Herwin Schaefer; Philip Roberts; Sonia Rolt for an extract from 'Thomas Newcomen: The Prehistory of the Steam Engine' by L T C Rolt published by David and Charles Ltd; Routledge & Kegan Paul Ltd for an extract from 'Family and Kinship in East London' by Michael Young and Peter Willmott; the Royal College of Art; Sir Gordon Russell for an extract from 'The Story of Furniture' published by Penguin Books Ltd; E F Schumacher for an extract from 'Survival of the Fitter' published in 'The Listener'; Studio Vista Publishers for an extract from 'The Nature of Design' by David Pye; T H White for an extract from 'The Once and Future King' published by William Collins Sons & Co Ltd; Wiley-Interscience for an extract from 'Design Methods' by J Christopher Jones.

All books are the result of team work. In that, they are exactly like design. I am fortunate to have had the help of such an excellent team.

Ken Baynes